THROUGH THE LOOKING GLASS OF GENEROSITY

THE CHURCH AS A GIFT

MICHAEL MOYNAGH

Published by

Fresh Expressions Limited 2025

freshexpressions.org.uk

godsend.cloud

© Michael Moynagh 2025

ISBN 9798311344524

ADDITIONAL COMMENDATIONS...

Gift and generosity are simple everyday ideas and pretty much everyone likes them. So what a great idea to explore the church in mission through the language of gift. It instantly invites the church into a...relation to the world which lets go of power and risks trusting the giving process.

Jonny Baker, Britain Hub Mission Director, CMS.

What a gift this book is...packed with examples and stories...with accessible theology clearly explained. Great to read, use and give to others.

David Cundill, Pioneer Development Officer, Diocese of Southwark.

This thought-provoking book challenges congregations to extend themselves beyond their walls...Rich in theology and practical insight.

Shannon Kiser, Senior Director, Fresh Expressions North America.

To Liz

CONTENTS

ACKNOWLEDGEMENTS   7

CHAPTER 1. A GIFT?   9

CHAPTER 2. A UNIQUE GIFT?   19

CHAPTER 3. WHAT'S THE GIFT LIKE?   29

CHAPTER 4. RECEIVING FIRST   41

CHAPTER 5. GIVING APPROPRIATELY   51

CHAPTER 6. LETTING GO   63

CHAPTER 7. ACCEPTING THE GIFT   75

CHAPTER 8. GIVING BACK   89

CHAPTER 9. TRANSFORMATION   101

CHAPTER 10. BEYOND HOSPITALITY   111

ACKNOWLEDGEMENTS

This is a much shorter, cheaper and hopefully more popular version of my book, *Giving the Church. The Christian Community through the Looking Glass of Generosity,* SCM, 2024, which was written for an academic audience. I am grateful again to all those who helped me with the first book, also to those who have commented favorably upon it, in particular to Simon Goddard and his team at Fresh Expressions who have designed and brought this version to publication, and once more to Liz for her unstinting and loving support. Shortcomings are, of course, mine.

1. A GiFT?

When Alice stepped through the looking glass, she entered a completely different world. This little book invites you to pass through a theological looking glass and totally re-imagine the people of God.

If you are starting a new Christian community, it offers you a framework to make sense of what you are doing.

If you are tired, bored with your Christian faith or despondent about the church, it suggests a vision to refresh your spirit and inject new energy into your Christian life.

If you are interested more broadly in what healthy giving looks like, this case study may encourage you to think about your own generosity. How might *your* giving be more considerate and kind?

1. THE THEME

As we gallop into an era where church and society feel poles apart, might generosity bridge the two? What if the church is a gift from God to others for the benefit of the world?

Now of course imagining and finding the right gift can be hard work. Sometimes we get it wrong and cause disappointment.

> **"A gift to others to benefit the world"**

But giving also brings joy. Indeed, presents are commonly linked with celebration. Think of birthdays and Christmases.

Or remember the banquet in Luke 14. 15-24. A rich man prepared a great feast and welcomed his friends. But they were too busy to come. So, he invited those on the edge of society – people who were poor and disabled.

Gourmet cuisine: what a gift to them!

A kingdom of generosity

Jesus said his reign – the kingdom of God – is like a free banquet. This is very different to human governments that pile on the burdens! God's reign is a gift.

Today we think of gifts as a form of altruism. You give something to please the recipient without seeking a benefit in return. Almost anything can be a gift, from an object to an action, to a contribution in a conversation.

Which means that God's reign can be a gift in a bonanza of ways – reconciliation, pastoral care, justice, creativity, beauty, creation care and more.

Above any other grouping, the church is to display what God's reign is like. It is to encapsulate the generosity of the kingdom by being a gift to others, a gift of festivity and merrymaking, a community in which presents are constantly and joyfully exchanged.

What if the church was like that – not a dutiful obligation, but a gift with a smile?

2. A GIFT FROM GOD

Generosity begins with God. One of the last century's great theologians, Hans Urs von Balthasar, said that giving lies at the heart of God.

If you ask what lies behind this generosity, the answer is more generosity. And if you look behind *that* generosity, what do you find? Even more generosity!

Keep digging and all you'll find is generosity.[1] Divine giving is a mineshaft without a bottom.

---

[1] Hans Urs von Balthasar, *The Glory of the Lord,* volume 1, Edinburgh: T. & T. Clark, 1982, p. 137.

Divine generosity breaks cover in the gift of creation, the gift of redemption, and – in a key ingredient of salvation – the gift of the church.

The church is a gift, but it also remains a possession. It is a 'people belonging to God' (1 Peter 2. 9). It's a treasure whose divine owner shares with others.

It's a gift like a sculpture on permanent loan to a gallery, or a soccer player loaned free to another club. God graciously cedes the right of use while retaining the rights of possession.

So, the church is not *ours* to give away. Because it belongs to God, we must first treat it with respect. The curator moves the sculpture with special care because it's on loan.

Equally, she shares it with the public because that is what the owner wishes. We give the church to others because that is what God desires.

3. A GIFT TO OTHERS

Is the church a gift mainly to its members? God pays for us to join God's club, which becomes a gift to us.

Given for a purpose

Now, the church *is* a gift in that sense. Christians are welcomed into the church, into a community built around Jesus.

But the gift is offered for a purpose. Believers receive community with Jesus not as an end in itself, but to share it with others.

The church is to be passed on. A gift is only a gift if it is offered to other people. A gift that is not shared ceases to be a gift and becomes a possession.

Perhaps a couple drink a gift of wine on their own instead of sharing the bottle with guests the next day. The gift is now a possession, consumed by its owners rather than given to others.

> **"A gift that is not shared becomes a possession"**

The church can never be a possession because it is the body of Christ. And Jesus is always a gift. He constantly shares what he has with the world. Just as Jesus is a perpetual gift, so must be the church.

Head and body together

Indeed, the church is the only human community that Scripture describes as Christ's body. Christ is the head and church the body. As such, the church must always travel in the same direction as its head. You cannot have the head walking north and the body going south.

From all eternity, Christ has been for humanity. That is why he became a human, died for the world, reigns over the cosmos, and is now working to bring *all* life to eternal joy.

If this is the path Christ treads, how can the church go a different way? Like Jesus who lives not for himself but for others, the church must be for the world. The church, too, must constantly give itself away.

Were its members to treat the church as their possession, the church would become a cul-de-sac for divine grace. God's generosity would pour into the church and then stop.

No longer would God's Son be given through the church to the world. Nor would the church play a role in reconciling 'all things' to Christ (Colossians 1. 20). Members would consume divine blessings for themselves.

Just as Jesus did not grasp the divinity he had been given by the Father (Philippians 2. 6-8), the church is not to cling to what it has received from God. All the church has is to be given away. The church is to be a gift to the world.

4. AN ATTRACTIVE GIFT?

This of course invites the objection: is the church a gift anyone would want to receive?

> **"The church's moral high ground has shrunk to a mole hill"**

Recent clerical child abuse and its cover up, the church's involvement in religious wars and genocide, the brutal internal politics of the church and more cast a noxious shadow over the claim to generosity. The church's moral high ground has shrunk to a mole hill.

Self-critique

Yet if the church as a gift sparks incredulity, might this not challenge God's people to become more attractive to others? 'What? Us? A gift! So…do we behave like a gift?'

Might the very call to be a gift invite the church to reflect critically on its life and prayerfully seek reform? And might this self-critique stop the church being given from a sense of superiority?

Instead, when they are offered to others, might God's people become a gift by standing:

- With those outside the church who have been shamed because the church itself has been shamed?
- With those who have abused their power because the church has also abused its power?
- With those who are anxious about their relevance because in many places the church, too, is anxious about its relevance?

A winsome humility

Just as friends may be gifts to one another by sharing their failures, might the church become a gift by standing in solidarity with others burdened by failure – 'you are not alone. We stand where you stand'?

And might this commend the church to a post-institutional age?

Many people are wary of the controlling nature of organizations. They want to be freed, valued and respected within supportive relationships, not have their strings pulled by bureaucratic puppeteers.

Can God's people be offered as something different – the gift of fulfilling relationships?

The church's manifold shortcomings may seem to say 'No.' Yet might the very transparency of a self-critical church, a church that publicly repents of its mistakes, build trust in the Christian community?

Could part of the answer to 'Why bother with church?' lie in combining honesty about the gift's defects with ambitions to be a more compelling gift? Might *this* be a church worth striving for?

5. FOR THE BENEFIT OF THE WORLD

The church is to be a particular type of gift. It belongs to the category of gifts that are offered for the sake of a third party.

When blood is donated, there is:

- The giver – the one who donates blood.
- The recipient – the hospital that receives the blood.
- The beneficiary – the patient who gets a blood transfusion.

Likewise, donors give to a charity and beneficiaries profit from the charity's work. The same should be true of the church. There will be the giver (God's people), the recipients (those who receive the church), and the beneficiaries.

These will be people who gain from the church's work – its pastoral care, evangelism, support for social and environmental justice, contributions to the creative arts (music and buildings for example), and so on.

> Members of *Bread Church*, a new Christian community, baked bread for their friends.
>
> *Knit and Natter* made prayer mats to give away.[2]
>
> An ecology group promotes a healthy environment.

The church is given to people beyond its walls, who serve people beyond the recipient group.

---

[2] Barbara Glasson, *Mixed-up Blessing: A New Encounter with Being Church,* Peterborough: Inspire, 2006; Christine Dutton, 'Unpicking Knit and Natter: Researching an Emerging Christian Community', *Ecclesial Practices* 1, 2014, pp. 31-50.

When the church is given for the benefit of the world, it becomes a more attractive gift.

6. SO GIVE IT AWAY!

All of which means that we must give the church away. If we have received the church as a gift from God, to be passed on to others, for the sake of the world, then we cannot remain in our pews. Prayerfully, we must live out what it means to be a gift to the world.

Not a second step

This can never be an afterthought. Giving the church cannot be a second step for God's people because generosity is not a second step for God.

Giving is fundamental to God's character. There has never been a 'time' when God's heart did not beat with a generous pulse. Otherwise, God would be inconsistent. God would change from not being generous to being generous.

And God is not like that. God is always the same (Hebrews 13. 8), always with generous plans for humanity (Ephesians 1. 4-5). Generosity is not a second step for God.

So, if the church is joined to God through Christ, generosity cannot be a second step for the church.

> **"Generosity must be the church's face"**

Generosity cannot be like makeup, applied only when God's people have worshipped, enjoyed fellowship, organized their life, and then want to go out.

Rather than being painted on to the face of God's people, generosity must be the face itself, constantly there, fundamental to the church as it is to God.

A continuous gift

Karl Barth, perhaps the last century's greatest theologian, went so far as to say that in every respect, even in what seems to be purely inner activity like prayer, worship, pastoral care and Bible study, the church must always be directed toward people outside.[3]

All the church does must focus ultimately on others.

This turns the church into a perpetual gift – a gift not like a box of chocolates you could enjoy on your own, but more like a traditional board game, which can be enjoyed only by being played with others.

The church is true to its head when it is 'played' with the world. If members enjoy the church as an end in itself, they are not playing church. They are playing another game.

DISCUSSION

1. What excites you about this chapter?
2. What reservations do you have?
3. What one thing would you like to think more about?

---

[3] Karl Barth, *Church Dogmatics, Volume IV, The Doctrine of Reconciliation,* Part 3.2, London: T&T Clark, 2004, p. 780.

2. A UNIQUE GIFT?

So, how can the church be a gift? And what does it mean for Christians to give the church to other people for the benefit of the world?

There are of course many ways for the church to be shared – or 'played' – with others. God's people can:

- Use their resources to serve others.
- Support campaigns for social and environmental justice.
- Become a dazzling beacon of what God is like through their life together.

- Describe their life with Jesus, just as friends share their experiences.

When the church acts in these ways, it behaves like many other organizations. They too become gifts by sharing their resources, putting themselves on display, and describing their experiences.

However, there is one gift that no other organization can offer, and that is the gift of communal life with Jesus. No one else can offer this particular gift; only the church, through the Spirit.

1. A PRECIOUS GIFT

When Christians share *this* gift, they offer to others the very essence of the church. That's because church happens when you encounter Jesus, when you encounter other people who have encountered Jesus, and when together you encounter the world. Church is a community centered on Christ.

A precious gift

Offering this communal life is a gift that is especially precious. It is one thing to share the gift of cinema tickets with a friend, quite another to share your life. Likewise, it is one thing for the church to share its resources, but quite another to share its heart, community with Jesus.

Indeed, when the church offers the crux of its life to other people, it follows the example of Jesus who gave his whole life for others.

This says something important about the church. Offering your life is a precious gift in the extreme. And the gift of something precious is a sign of how much you love the recipient.

A statement of love

So, to give away communal life with Jesus is to make a vivid statement about the extent of the church's love for the world.

> **"The church is to give its inside to people on the outside"**

Which means it is not enough to campaign for justice or to lovingly serve other people, hugely important though these are. The church is to go further: like Jesus, it is to offer its very life, the core of its existence, which is community with Christ.

The church is to give its inside to people on the outside.

2. A GIFT OF CHRIST

Some might say this downplays the gift of Jesus. Isn't this even more important than the gift of the church?

The answer is that you cannot separate the two. Because Jesus has made his followers his family, he cannot be cut adrift from them. 'My mother and my siblings are those who hear the word of God and do it' (Luke 8. 21). Believers are 'one in Christ' (Galatians 3. 28).

In other words, the risen Lord would not be who he is without his human community, like I would not be a Moynagh without my family. Just as you cannot have Christ without his heavenly community, Father, Son and Spirit, you cannot have Christ without his earthly community, the church.

Of course, someone might wish to connect with Jesus but not his family, just as they might wish to befriend me but not my relatives.

> "Christ's earthly community belongs as much to him as his heavenly community"

However, if – as in some cultures – my hospitality always included members of my family ('Come to supper' means eating with the family), they would join me in hanging out with them. To accept my hospitality would be to accept my relations.

Likewise, to receive the gift of Christ is not to receive him as a solitary divine person. Nor is it first to accept Jesus in your heart and then, later, receive the church. It is to receive all others in Christ *at the very same time* as you receive him. We are adopted not into a divine person but a divine family.

This in no way diminishes the supremacy of Christ. It simply describes his identity. This is who Jesus is – the head of the church. To receive the gift of Christ is to receive the gift of being with him, in community.

3. IN THE FORM OF NEW CHRISTIAN COMMUNITIES

The church is called to give away its very *self*, community with Jesus. But what does this involve?

In some cases, the gift will be fruitfully offered through an invitation to an existing congregation. But for many people, such an invitation will be inappropriate.

The existing congregation may be out of reach because of when, where and how it meets. A gift is not a gift if you cannot receive it.

An exclusive church

Here is something that many people forget: every congregation is exclusive by nature. Once you have decided to meet at a particular time, in a particular place, with a certain agenda and a certain style, you will attract some people, but you are bound to put off many others.

You will exclude all those

- Who cannot come at that time for work, family or other reasons.
- Who cannot access the church because of their disabilities or where they live.
- Who do not share your agenda to worship Christ.
- Who find the style a turn-off (maybe they think sermons spell hierarchy and are relics of a past age).

A congregation is a group. And 'from an anthropological perspective, if there is no homogeneity, there is no groupness.'[4]

Groups thrive if they have something in common – culture, similar background, a shared interest, and so on. This affinity attracts some people but deters others. 'I've got nothing in common with them.'

As a type of group, congregations by necessity are exclusive.

---

[4] Charles H. Kraft, 'An anthropological apologetic for the homogeneous unit principle in missiology', *International Bulletin of Mission Research,* 2 (4) 1978, p. 121.

Which means, incidentally, that they have the character of gifts. A gift is offered to some people, but not others. I give a present to the birthday boy, but not his sister. Each congregation was originally given to a particular group of people.

It follows that as a gift from God to the world, the church will inevitably be passed on to certain people but not at the same time to everyone.

From exclusion to inclusion

This is a big problem. We worship an *inclusive* God, who died on the cross with his arms outstretched in a welcome to everybody. But we worship this God in *exclusive* congregations.

How can we square the circle? How can we offer an exclusive gift to all people?

A promising answer is to start new Christian communities at a time and place, with an agenda and style that *do* connect with people for whom the church is currently inaccessible.

These will not be 'wild west' solo ventures. Typically, they will connect to their parent congregation or church. They will be congregations of the parish church, or worshipping communities linked to their local congregation.

These new communities are an ideal way to serve the *entire* neighborhood. The more the church is passed on to one demographic, then the next, and then the next again, the more a tide of love will flood the terrain.

> Wildwood United Methodist Church in Florida started 14 new communities between 2012 and 2020. They were intended to become worshipping communities and were among dog walkers, young professionals, families, people in recovery, health enthusiasts, past and present drug dealers, and more.
>
> A small, struggling church in a poor neighborhood avoided a slow death by giving itself in multiple communities to ever more people beyond its doors.

4. VITAL FOR OUTREACH

New Christian communities can support almost every calling within the galactic scope of God's mission.

Support for any missional agenda

If it is discipleship at work, we have examples of these communities serving an office, a school and patients of a medical practice.

> One Methodist chaplain got to know fellow workers over lunch. They began discussing topics in the news. The group grew so large that management offered them a room to meet. The conversations gradually

> acquired a spiritual hue – the beginnings perhaps of a new Christian community.

If the priority is a specific group – homeless people, abused women, asylum seekers, gay people, teenagers in a run-down neighborhood, or people with learning difficulties – a small team can listen to them, love and serve them, build relationships with them, introduce those interested to Jesus, and encourage a Christian community to emerge. In South Africa, a woman described how she was doing this among sex workers.

If the focus is the environment, social justice or global poverty, Christians can listen to people outside the church who share their concern, find ways of working together, form community as they do so, and explore how Christian spirituality can make a contribution.

> One rural church formed an ecology group with people who did not normally attend church. Short spiritual devotions on creation and other environmental themes opened the door to further conversations about God.

New Christian communities can input into the entire panorama of mission not by taking a concern over, nor by smugly assuming that 'we've got it together,' but by offering community with Jesus in humble support of the group's objectives.

Potentially, there is no square inch of mission to which a new Christian community cannot contribute – a big claim!

Share your passion

The same applies to individuals. Whatever passion you have

– sport, photography, craft, walking, singing, Minecraft – there could be an opportunity to

- share it with others,

- grow community with them,
- describe your life with Jesus as relationships deepen, and
- encourage the willing to start a new Christian community where they are.

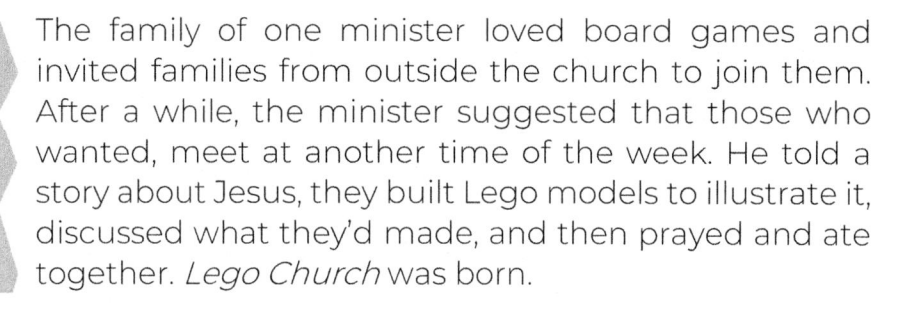

> The family of one minister loved board games and invited families from outside the church to join them. After a while, the minister suggested that those who wanted, meet at another time of the week. He told a story about Jesus, they built Lego models to illustrate it, discussed what they'd made, and then prayed and ate together. *Lego Church* was born.

5. SO START A NEW COMMUNITY!

Share your interests with people who don't usually attend church. Maybe you love films. Why not start a film club 'with a spiritual dimension' among your neighbors?

Watch a favorite video one evening and host a bring-and-share supper on another. Over the meal, discuss the film from a spiritual and ethical angle.

At the end, perhaps, include a short 'spiritual extra' (elements of worship and prayer) for those who want. cofe.io/soulspace shows how easy and non-threatening this can be. Click, download, and off you go!

Over time, deepen the spiritual content in ways that *Soulspace* suggests. A new Christian community will imperceptibly emerge around films, based on Jesus. (godsend.cloud has lots of other ideas.)

Do this and through the Holy Spirit:

- Your faith will relate more strongly to your daily life.
- You'll find a practical way to love people around you.
- New people will receive community with Jesus and connect to the wider church, making God's people more inclusive.
- The church's gifts to the world will multiply as new believers stuff their time, talents and money into the church's year-round Christmas stocking.

Giving away communion with Christ will grow your faith, demonstrate godly love, make God's people more welcoming, and multiply the church's generosity to others. What's not to like!

DISCUSSION

1. What interests and passions might you share with people outside the church?
2. Might you add a 'spiritual extra' (elements of worship and prayer) to an outreach activity run by your church?
3. If so, could cofe.io/soulspace be a help?

3. WHAT'S THE GIFT LIKE?

God's people are a gift to others for the benefit of the world. Christians can share this gift in many ways, but especially by offering new Christian communities. So, what do these communities look like? When the gift is unwrapped, what's inside?

Many people assume a new Christian community – a new congregation in effect – will be similar to their existing congregation. Their experience of church is so deeply engrained that they cannot imagine anything else.

Yet the cultural valley between today's congregations and people outside is often immense. Canyons of language, music, assumptions about life and more, put many congregations out of reach.

> **"The cultural valley is often immense"**

Think of it like this. In the past, classrooms were arranged in rigid rows. Now pupils sit in flexible groups of varying sizes. Yet most congregations are still in the era of rows. They haven't adapted to people who prefer circles to lines.

This is why some Christians have been experimenting with new types of congregations, from Messy Church to Minecraft Church, from Craft Church to Cafe Church, from Sewing Church to Sports Church.

But is this proper church?

A quick thought will show that 'my' congregation isn't necessarily the norm. Across the world congregations are astonishingly varied:

- From cathedrals to churches-in-the-home.
- From gatherings round the altar, to those round the pulpit, to those round the music stand.
- From rigid 'North Koreans' of church to slightly chaotic 'Italians'.
- From churches that see mission as social action to those which concentrate on evangelism.
- From 'progressive' to more 'conservative' congregations.

Remember: at Christmas we don't all give each other the same gifts. Different gifts suit different people. So it is with the church. The gift looks different in different settings.

So what do these different shapes have in common? What makes them church?

1. RELATIONSHIP COMES FIRST

It's tempting to answer that church is what we *do*. 'We celebrate the sacraments,' 'We put ourselves under the word,' 'We encounter the Spirit,' 'We engage in mission,' perhaps even 'We argue a lot!'

What is identity?

Now, these and other practices *are* important. But more important are relationships. Identity is defined by connections with people.

As one of today's leading theologians, Rowan Williams, remarked: 'Who we are becomes clear to those around when we put ourselves in a map of relationships.'[5]

My identity is shaped by my family, by being British, by the football team I support, by whether and where I work, and by so much more – above all, by being a follower of Christ. All these at their root are relationships.

And the same is true of the church's identity. The church is fundamentally about connections. What the church does springs from and contributes to its various relationships.

When for example a congregation gathers to worship (what it does), members interact with God, with each other and, through their prayers, with the communion of saints and the world. Relationships form and deepen.

---

[5] Rowan Williams, 'Christian Identity and Religious Pluralism', Address to World Council of Churches Assembly, Porto Alegre, 17 February 2006.

Practices build relationships

An emphasis on relationships avoids making practices like studying the Bible and celebrating Holy Communion ends in themselves. Basing the church's identity on what the church does makes it easy to say, 'If we celebrate the sacraments, preach the word and so forth, the job's done.' But it's not.

Holy Communion and Scripture are for a purpose: to strengthen relationships with God, the world and fellow Christians. 'Everything must be done so that the church' – members and their networks – 'may be built up' (1 Corinthians 14.26).

If sermons and sacraments fail in that, something is wrong. Perhaps they have become too mechanical or are not connected with people's lives.

Practices contain relationships

Worship, outreach, fellowship and other practices of the church *are* crucial. The church's relationships could not exist without them, just as relationships in a basketball team would not exist without the sport.

Activities are receptacles for social bonds. Take the container away, and relationships would crumble through lack of support.

However, the container is not the connection itself. A married couple might find that a daily walk strengthens their union. But their marriage cannot be reduced to activities like walking. It is what the couple do *within* the activity that counts. Does the walk become an arena of destructive conflict?

Likewise, what God's people do creates vessels for relating together, but these containers are not the essence of the church's relational life.

That's why many of the New Testament descriptions of the church have relationships, not practices, at their heart. Think of the household of God (1 Timothy 3.15), body of Christ (Romans 12.5), and the vine and the branches (John 15.5). Relationships are the starting blocks of church.

2. FOUR SETS OF RELATIONSHIPS

Specifically, what defines the church are four overlapping sets of relationships, all centered on Jesus: with God directly in prayer, worship and study; with the wider church; with the outside world; and within the congregation itself. No other community or organization has these particular connections.

In the Corinthian church for example:

- Members experienced God directly
  (1 Corinthians 12.7-11).
- They connected to other Christian communities; members read Paul's letters and looked up to leaders in the church at large (1 Corinthians 1.12).
- They engaged with the outside world
  (1 Corinthians 14.23-25).
- They related to each other in worship
  (1 Corinthians 14.26-31).

These overlapping sets of relationships are equally important. That's because Jesus is central to each of them, and together they make for a balanced and healthy community.

You might think that the relationship with God should be pre-eminent. But God is equally involved in all four sets of relations. What distinguishes the first is the connection *directly* with God through prayer, study and worship.

So we shouldn't emphasize one set of relationships over the others. In particular, we must not think that ties within the congregation are more important than relations with the wider church. Connections to the whole church may consume less of our time but they don't consume less of God's time!

In 1 Corinthians 12 Paul stresses that *all* parts of the body are to be equally valued.

3. FOUR SETS OF PRACTICES

So where do Bible study, sacraments and other vital activities fit in? Christians have traditionally seen at least some of these as being fundamental to the church.

You can think about this by distinguishing between the *essence* of the church and what is *essential* for the church. The two need not be the same.

A referee is essential for a soccer match but is not the essence of the game. In the West, a knife and fork are essential for eating but are not the essence of the meal. The cup is essential for the wine to be distributed at Holy Communion but is not the essence of what is shared.

The essentials

If four sets of relationships are the essence of church, four overlapping sets of practice are essential for the church. These are:

- the word (Bible study and preaching for example),
- the sacraments (of baptism and Holy Communion),

- ministry (leadership shared with church members), and
- disciplines (meeting together and other spiritual habits).

These essentials originated in the church's relationships. They arose from interactions within the community that Jesus founded. And ever since the Holy Spirit has worked through them to knit the church's social threads.

Avenues of the Spirit

The essentials are vehicles of the Spirit, who uses them to soak the four relationships in divine generosity.

When this happens, the essentials of word, sacrament, ministry and disciplines become:

- *Instruments* through which Christians are enabled to receive God's gifts and pass them on.
- *Sites* in which generosity in the four sets of connection can be experienced. For example, gathering around the word, sacraments, godly leaders and shared spiritual habits can enable church members to experience God's grace directly, to receive treasures from the Christian heritage, to be equipped to serve the world, and to be enriched by gifts shared within the congregation.
- *Prerequisites* for the church. A feature of many 'essentials' is that they precede 'essences'. The cup is present before being filled with wine. Just as the cup enables the distribution, word, sacraments, ministry and disciplines enable the church.

In other words, the essentials are not optional extras. They are *essentials*. Word, sacraments, ministry and disciplines are crucial for the church. They are the trellis on which the four sets of relationships grow.

4. WHAT CAN CHANGE AND WHAT CAN STAY THE SAME?

All this means that church can look very different in different contexts. When you offer community with Jesus to people outside the church, you don't have to pass on a replica of your existing congregation.

Like an artist might paint different portraits as gifts to two friends, the church can be given in a variety of forms to fit different people. The church will be a welcome gift when it respects others' uniqueness.

Same and different

What must always stay the same is the presence of the church's four overlapping sets of relationships. No community can be God's people without deepening its connections with God directly, with the wider church, with the world and within the gathering itself.

Equally, what must also be present are the four essentials – word, sacraments, ministry and disciplines. Without these, the church's networks cannot be 'in Christ'.

Within a tradition's understanding of the essentials, however, what can change are the practices that are included, the significance attached to them and how they are expressed – for example:

- How the word is preached (through discussion for instance) and for how long (does it send you to sleep?).
- How Communion is celebrated and its frequency.

- How ministry is exercised and shared.
- What disciplines are encouraged and how.

The Church of England, for example, understands the church as congregations in which the word is preached and the sacraments are celebrated by duly authorized ministers, using authorized liturgies.

The word, sacraments (Baptism and Holy Communion), ministry (bishops, priests and deacons) and disciplines (authorized liturgies) are given concrete form in an Anglican manner. Other traditions bring the essentials to life in *their* ways.

> "One hand can wear a multitude of gloves"

What matters is that the essentials serve the relationships. Word, sacraments, ministry and disciplines should take a form that best builds up the church's four overlapping sets of relationship. Essentials should fit the relational context.

That's why they can vary. One hand can wear a multitude of gloves.

Recognition

The four relationships and four essential practices can help you to recognize when a new initiative has evolved into a congregation. Say you start a foodbank. Then you add a community meal before the foodbank opens. When would the meal become a new Christian community (or congregation)?

Might we say this: new communities lacking any of the four sets of relationship are '*on their way to being church*'?

Communities that have begun to grow in these relationships but haven't embraced all four essentials are '*beginning to be church*.' They are paddling in the shallow end of the church, where 'ecclesial grace' extends to those involved.[6]

As communities wade further into the deeper end and embrace all the essentials, they will be '*completely church*' (though perhaps not mature church).

They will receive more abundant grace, be empowered to express the church more fully, and be drawn more strongly toward the coming kingdom. Progressive recognition – more and more rather than either/or – would affirm the community on its journey and encourage members to keep pressing on.

But what if you want a short answer to 'Is it now church?', 'Has it arrived as a congregation?' Well, the reply is 'Yes' if the initiative is growing into the four sets of relationships that comprise the swimming pool, and if it has the four essentials that enable you to swim in the deep end.

A pathway to a new congregation

1. Add an *optional* 10-minute spiritual extra (elements of worship and prayer), such as 'Soulspace', to an outreach activity – light a candle, play some music, read an appropriate Bible passage, have a short headspace ('to pray to God as you understand God, or have positive thoughts for a person or situation'), conclude with a short poem or prayer.

2. When there's an appetite, include a short discussion about the reading to grow the optional extra into a

---

[6] This metaphor is used by Clare Watkins and Bridget Shepherd, 'The challenge of "Fresh Expressions" to ecclesiology. Reflections from the practice of messy church', *Ecclesial Practices,* 1 (2014), pp. 92-110.

'church service', with Welcome, Worship through music, Bible reading, Sermon in the form of discussion, silent Prayer, Blessing.

3. Then add in a Confession, short Creed and Lord's Prayer to make it (in Church of England language) a Service of the Word.

4. Finally, add a short Eucharistic Prayer, leading to a new congregation with full sacramental worship.

Pray that people encounter Jesus along the way and are drawn into relationship with him.

Go to cofe.io/soulspace for orders of service and resources to help you on your way. A few clicks and you're ready to go!

5. WHAT ARE THE TAKE-AWAYS?

First, when we give the church to others, the content of the gift is the four overlapping sets of relationships and the four essential sets of practices.

Secondly, new types of Christian community for new places and people will only be 'church' if they have these relationships and practices.

Thirdly, these relationships and practices may look very different. A new congregation need not replicate an old one. It may be light years from what you are used to.

But it can still be 'church' if it has the four sets of relationships and the four sets of practices. Each new community must fit the recipients, otherwise it won't make sense to them.

When you offer the church, you don't give away a Lego model. You give the Lego bricks. Prepare to be surprised by how the bricks are put together!

DISCUSSION

1. When you think of the church, which sets of relationships first spring to mind? How much attention do you pay to the other relationships?

2. Imagine a group of people you would love to serve. What might a new Christian community look like for them? How would it be different from, and how would it be similar to the congregation where you currently worship?

3. Imagine this new community comes to birth. Which of the four sets of relationships would be most difficult to grow? What might help in growing them?

4. Try the short version of Soulspace. Could you use it with any of your outreach groups or your networks?

4. RECEIVING FIRST

Christians are called to offer the church's self, community with Christ, to others for the sake of the world. Often this gift will take the form of new Christian communities centered on four overlapping sets of relationships, enabled by four essential sets of practices.

But can these communities be a welcome gift? Much depends on *how* they are offered. In some languages, 'gift' and 'poison' come from the same root!

Oscar Wilde probably best described the potential nastiness of giving. In 1891 he blisteringly complained that charity degrades and demoralizes its objects. It reinforces the status quo by reconciling the poor to their poverty. And it exerts control by coming with strings attached.[7]

Yet need offering communal life with Christ be quite so bleak? Might it escape ethical gloom by being framed with the life and witness of Jesus?

Using the gift of new Christian communities as an example, I want to suggest six practices that will light up any form of generosity.

The first is receiving before you give.

1. INCREASING THE CAPACITY TO GIVE

Christ is a gift from God to the world (John 3. 16). As such, Jesus encapsulates what being a gift should involve. Not least, he shows that being a gift starts with receiving.

Jesus received first

Jesus received his humanity before he gave his life. As an infant, he received from his parents before intentionally giving back to them. As an adolescent, he received from his surrounding culture before he pitched fresh insights into it (Luke 2. 41-52). And in his public ministry, time and again he accepted others' hospitality before offering them his kingdom gifts.

---

[7] Oscar Wilde, *The Soul of Man under Socialism,* Whitefish, MT: Kessinger Publishing, 2004 (1891).

To be a gift in the slipstream of Jesus, the church too must be a recipient before it is a giver – for three reasons.

Having more to give

First, receiving before giving turns up the capacity to give. You can offer a gift only if you've got the necessary resources. You must either own the gift, have the materials and skills to make the gift, or possess the money to buy it.

> **"The more the church receives, the more it can give"**

'We can give because we have first received from others.'[8] Without abilities endowed at birth, blessings of nurture and care, and payments of various kind, we would have nothing to give.

And this is true of the church. God's people must receive from others if they are to give to them. Indeed, the more the church receives the fruits of God's activity in the world, the more it can give the world the fruits of God's activity in the church.

Receiving may hurt

In particular, the world's gifts may include uncomfortable criticisms of the church. Complaints may home in on sexual abuse, other perversions of power, pastoral neglect, insensitive evangelism, an arrogant superiority, or meanness of heart.

---

[8] Antonio Malo, 'The limits of Marion's and Derrida's philosophy of the gift', *International Philosophical Quarterly,* 52 (2), 2012, p. 165.

These rebukes may hurt, but they can also become gifts by bringing the church to repentance. The church can then celebrate God's forgiveness by requesting a further gift: help from the world in addressing their shortcomings.

Learning from the world about safeguarding, non-coercive leadership, and respect for difference are gifts that the church often takes for granted. But God's people will become a better gift when they joyfully welcome these presents – when they relish the Spirit's activity *outside* the church.

2. BRINGING OUT THE BEST

Secondly, receiving before giving locates generosity within a mutual, two-way relationship. It provides a counterblast to paternalism.

So often the church thinks that loving people means doing things *for* them. Yet elite acts of love include allowing people to do things for *us*, because when people give, they are enabled to flourish.

A neighbor who gives me a meal can express their cooking abilities. A friend who takes me to an athletics event can share their knowledge of athletics. Someone who drives me to the hospital can practice their concern.

> **"Love reveals people at their best"**

Indeed, almost by definition any act of giving is an opportunity to love. And when people show love, they reveal themselves at their best.

That is why one of the greatest gifts of God's people is to allow others to be generous to them (without reducing this to intrusive fund-raising). For in the act of giving, the person puts their better side on display.

When he encountered Zacchaeus, Jesus did not shame him for his misdeeds. He healed him by asking for a kindness. Shame was countered by acceptance, isolation by conviviality, and embarrassment by joy.

Christ wins gold for generosity, and by giving chase the church can join him on the podium.

3. GIVING FREEDOM

Thirdly, receiving first inverts the power dynamics of giving. For generosity is fraught with difficulty. Being the first to give can be a threat. Giving invites a return gift, an obligation that may feel like an imposition. It also invites a relationship, and the recipient may not be ready for that.

Receiving before giving on the other hand, transforms the direction of obligation. Instead of the church's generosity putting the world under a duty to respond, the world's giving places a duty on the church.

Shifting the power balance

For example, perhaps a congregation sends a team to start a new Christian community in an apartment block. Some of the team move in and find they need to do some repairs. Rather than asking their friends for help, they turn to people next door. 'Let's be good neighbors' is their implied request.

Yet despite being dab hands at DIY, the occupants claim they would love to help but are pressed for time. Suspicious of newcomers, they hold back till they know the new arrivals better. Their excuse is plausible, so they can decline without appearing rude.

Equally, by reducing the uncertainty in giving, the request makes it easier for the neighbors to initiate friendliness if they wish. They needn't worry that a welcome gift out of the blue would seem too forward, nor what sort of gift would be appropriate. They can provide help, knowing it will be gratefully received.

However, having asked for help and freed their neighbors to start the gift exchange, the churchgoers will not have the same freedom in whether to respond. To avoid appearing ungrateful, they must return the gift at some stage. To an extent, their hands are tied. They must give a present as a 'thank you.'

'Whereas the initial gift may be voluntary, the counter-gift can only ever be given out of obligation.'[9] If the world chooses to give to the church, good manners require the church to give in response; the *church* is placed under an obligation.

Giving the initiative away

But the original givers are still free. They were asked to help, they responded, the new arrivals have shown gratitude, and the giving and receiving seesaw is now level.

If they want, the first givers can view the exchange as complete. They need not offer another gift unless they wish to maintain and develop the relationship. Once more, the initiative is in their hands.

The church tilts the power balance toward the world by placing itself in the world's debt. And because gratitude can arise from dependence on others, it is the *church* that feels the slight discomfort of being under an obligation. God's

---

[9] Rebecca Colesworthy, *Returning the Gift: Modernism and the thought of exchange,* Oxford: Oxford University Press, 2018, p. 183.

people trade their autonomy for a relationship on equal terms.

This helps to avoid a high-horse approach to mission: Christians benevolently sacrifice their time and resources for the benefit of other people, who are seen through the lens of their needs.

> **"The church trades its autonomy for a relationship on equal terms"**

Instead, others are not treated as passive *recipients* of mission, but as active *participants*; the Spirit is already at work in them, and they have gifts from God to bring.

They are not *objects* to be converted, but *persons* with riches to share. As they bless the church, maybe the church will have a chance to share Christ and bless them?

Becoming like Christ

Here then is a big difference between the church and its head. Christ is always the first giver, whereas the church best resists its sinful arrogance by being first to receive.

Yet paradoxically, by receiving first, the church also becomes a giver. It acquires the resources to give. It offers others the gift of an opportunity to put their better sides on display. And it frees the world from being obligated to return the church's gift.

So remarkably, when humans are humble enough to first receive (showing their difference to God), what happens? They become more like God!

4. LISTENING FIRST

In the context of giving the church away, what does receiving first involve? More than anything it's about listening:

- To God.
- To the people you are called to serve.
- To others with helpful experience.

Through listening you receive gifts of information, advice and offers to help.

Drinks in Dundee

Hot Chocolate began with Christians giving cups of hot chocolate to young people in Dundee city centre, Scotland. The Christians discovered that the teenagers wanted somewhere to play music.

So, they opened the church building, got to know the young people, loved them in all sorts of ways, built relationships with them and shared the gospel.

From this emerged a new Christian community that served hundreds of young people and was still thriving 20 years later.

It started with listening.

Did you know that in the gospels Jesus is 40 times more likely to ask a question than to give an answer? Jesus asked 307 questions but gave straight answers to only eight![10]

---

[10] Martin B. Copenhaver, *Jesus is the Question. The 307 questions Jesus asked and the three he answered,* Nashville, TN: Abingdon, 2014, p. xviii. Copenhaver cites two studies suggesting Jesus gave only 3 direct replies but thinks that a maximum of 8 is more accurate.

The church must mirror Jesus to connect deeply with the people it serves. It must make itself vulnerable by exposing its ignorance and by inviting others to fill the gaps. It must listen especially to voices that are unheard by people with influence, and to voices within individuals that are too hurt to speak.

> **"Jesus asked 307 questions but answered only eight!"**

Listening can balm bruises that ache. So, the better the church listens, the closer it can link arms with people on the social edge. It can ease distress through empathetic solidarity.

Self-awareness

The church is called to show the world what healthy giving is like. The starting point is to receive first. And this requires an attentive ear.

To be beacons of good listening, God's people must tune in to themselves. They must notice their words – whether their speech asserts control or unleashes others' potential.

- Are they manipulating conversations by steering what gets discussed and what doesn't?
- Do their confident contributions intimidate others?
- Do their claims include facts, use arguments and employ language that their audience would consider fair?
- Are they limiting their contributions to leave plenty of space for others'?

- Do other people leave the conversation with hearts aglow through their encounter with the church?

Self-awareness – critical self-examination – is the foundation for a spirituality of giving. It is the clothes rail on which listening hangs. Good listening energizes receiving first. And receiving first puts the church's humility on public display.

As Cambridge psychologist, Sara Savage, said: 'The experience of being listened to well is as close to the experience of being loved as to make no difference.'

DISCUSSION

1. What have been some of your good and bad experiences of receiving generosity?

2. Think of some people you don't know well. What might be the equivalent of giving them cups of hot chocolate?

3. What would be appropriate for you to ask from them?

5. GIVING APPROPRIATELY

We are thinking about healthy giving – what it looks like. And as an example, we are asking how the church can become an attractive gift through the way it offers itself – as a community with Christ – to others.

The first step, receiving before giving, is itself a gift, a powerful expression of love. So too is the next step – giving appropriately.

1. THINK OF JESUS

Jesus was a fitting gift. He came as a human, and so revealed God in a form that women and men can understand. The gift was appropriate to the recipients.

Yet the gift was also faithful to the giver, Jesus's heavenly Father. Jesus was both human and divine; he retained the divinity that 'proceeded' from his Father. In other words, his Father's divine nature was embedded in the gift.

Jesus's combination of these human and divine natures, distinct but one, bridges the gulf between God and humanity. It makes possible an appropriate relationship between the two.

Christ therefore modeled what is typical of healthy gifts. Gifts are appropriate to the recipient, to the giver, and to the relationship between them.

2. APPROPRIATE TO THE RECIPIENT

A present would not be much of a gift if it was unsuitable. A friend who was teetotal would hardly welcome a bottle of wine.

To be received with pleasure, a gift must be the 'right fit' for the recipient. It must enhance the person's life.

So, when the church offers communion in Christ, the character and shape of the community will chime with the best interests of those who receive it. The community will be:

- *Accessible.* It will be culturally and physically close to recipients so that they can take hold of it.
- *Engaging.* Its style and agenda will resonate with them.
- *Enriching.* It will help them enjoy a fuller life and realize their potential.
- *Pleasing.* When recipients unwrap the gift, they will delight in it.

- *Surprising.* It will be more than the receiver could have expected.

This will be a far cry from manipulative giving controlled by the *giver's* desires. It will be generosity that puts the *recipient* first; the church travels along the rail tracks of other people's lives. Might this be quietly endearing?

A spiritual discipline

To give appropriately, the church must pay careful attention to the recipients – to their longings, needs, character and riches.

You can think of this as a form of prayer. Through contemplation, the Spirit etches recipients on the minds of God's people and steers their thinking, just as an emerging story impresses itself on the novelist and directs what the author seeks to write.

In the light of Christ, a picture forms of those to whom the church wishes to give, and – as with all gifts – the picture will be conveyed in the nature of the gift.

Contextual giving

When this happens, giving becomes contextual. The gift fits a niche within the cultural expectations of those who receive it.

> **"Gifts add a distinctive song"**

This doesn't mean givers lose their distinctiveness. For good gifts add something new to their recipients. They are gifts precisely because they bring something extra. Stamp enthusiasts welcome *additions* to their collection.

So, the gift of a new Christian community will not be stuck on the same note as recipients. It will add a distinctive song, a song inspired by Jesus's open arms to others. It will embrace the setting in which recipients live and bring something beautiful to it.

Welcome in Milton Keynes

A church in Milton Keynes, England took to heart the food poverty of its neighborhood by starting a foodbank. When long queues formed, it opened its arms more widely and offered a free lunch.

Then it realized that some people were hungry for spiritual food. So, it included an optional devotion during the meal.

After this was well received, it opened its arms still further and invited the willing to an exploratory Bible study before the lunch. The hope is that this will become a new congregation, connected to the parent church.

At each stage the church blended into the landscape while adding an inviting detail.

3. APPROPRIATE TO THE GIVER

Writers on giving have long said that gifts reveal something about the giver. As the American Ralph Emerson famously put it, a person's biography is conveyed in their gift.[11]

When some of my family visited an exhibition of presents given to the royal family, we were struck by how many made a statement about the giver.

For example, there was a beautiful gift of three gold palm trees and a camel. Where was it from? Saudi Arabia.

---

[11] Ralph Waldo Emerson, 'Gifts' in Edna H. L. Turpin (ed.), *Essays by Ralph Waldo Emerson,* New York: Charles E. Merrill, 1907.

Givers in their gifts

Gifts reflect the thought (or lack of it) that went into choosing or making the gift, and this thought accompanies the gift when it is handed over. The more care put into the present, the more the giver's self will be in the gift.

'Why did they bring such a cheap wine?' the hosts complain after the guests leave. 'I guess they don't think much of us.' A giver isn't just proving her magnanimity. She is making a statement about herself, her view of the recipient and how she sees the relationship.[12]

When Jesus turned water into wine at a wedding, the wine was admired for its quality (John 2. 10). By holding nothing back, Jesus revealed something of his generosity. The miracle was an authentic gift because it expressed his identity, the divine gift.

Honest gifts

Similarly, the church's gift of a new Christian community must accurately convey who the church is. Through the Spirit, the gift must truthfully reflect the church's character as *God's* people.

This authenticity must also be true of particular traditions within the church. Each will offer a new community with the fingerprints of the tradition's history with Christ. For example:

- A denomination will pray that in time the new community will identify with its story and contribute to it.
- A local church will build on its strengths. One person who started a language cafe for recent

---

[12] Mark Osteen, 'Gift or commodity?' in Mark Osteen (ed.), *The Question of the Gift. Essays across disciplines,* Abingdon: Routledge, 2002, p. 23.

immigrants said to her congregation: 'For years we have supported mission overseas. Now overseas has come to us! What are we going to do about it?'

- A team will share its passions and interests and wait for the Spirit to use this act of love to open participants' hearts to Christ.

For instance, a minister enjoys Minecraft. So he invites teenagers from the neighborhood to bring their phones and tablets, sit on bean bags in the local hall, eat lots of snacks and play Minecraft together.

As they chat, spiritual themes come up, such as anger and forgiveness, meaning and purpose, health and wellbeing. Often he'll ask the young people to model a theme in Minecraft.

Forgiveness might be a scene of destruction: memory of the event is blown up. Bible stories and prayers can be built.

'It's easy!' he said. 'The young people come up with the ideas.' He enjoys the experience as much as them.

His prayer is that this will become 'Minecraft Church' in which everyone is blessed, including himself.

The start was his passion. The initiative is not a burdensome extra, imposed by the church and severing him from his joys. *His* signature is on the gift.

And this must be true of all the church's gifts. They must be signed by the giver – the denomination, the local church, and the founding team.

Which may prompt God's people to ask: if it is *our* signature, what does the gift say about us? Are we the sort of people others would be pleased to receive?

4. APPROPRIATE TO THE RELATIONSHIP

A gift must suit not only the recipient and the giver, but also the relationship between them. You don't expect the same from close friends and slight acquaintances, or from lovers and your godmother.[13]

So, when the church prays to be a gift to others, it will ask: 'What would be a celebratory thing to say about our relationship at this stage?'

It follows that God's people will pause before offering community with Jesus till the relationship can bear the weight (see Matthew 7. 6).

Speaking volumes

Remember: community with Christ is an especially valuable gift. If the church is a gathering around Jesus, you cannot get closer to the church's self than that.

---

[13] Helmuth Berking, *Sociology of Giving,* London: Sage, 1999, pp. 4-5.

So, offering community with Jesus means bestowing the very heart of the church's life. And for givers, no gift can be more precious than their life.

Handing over the church's life makes a huge statement. It says how much the church esteems the recipients. Precious gifts are reserved for precious people.

However, a gift that assumes its recipients are cherished will be an honest form of communication only if the recipients have been treated as such. And that may take time.

No strings attached

The likely starting point will be a venture of love with no spiritual conditions attached, such as a community meal for people who are lonely, a grief group for sufferers of loss, or bringing to life a shared passion like walking, skateboarding or films; love is shown by creating a platform for mutual enjoyment and support.

As people gather around the activity, stepping stones to faith may look like this:

- *From hostility to distrust.* 'I'll come, but I don't trust the church.'

- *From distrust to indifference.* 'The leaders are OK, but I'm not interested in Christ.'

- *From indifference to curiosity.* 'Jesus seems interesting.'

- *From curiosity to openness.* 'Maybe Christ is for me.'

- *From openness to active seeking.* 'I want to explore Jesus.'

- *From seeking to joining.* 'I want to follow Jesus.'

- *From joining to growing.* 'How can I live more like Christ?'

This is not about herding people into categories. It's about forming community that is sensitive to people's different spiritual outlooks.

It is about respecting where people are on the pathway, refusing to pressurize them into a further step, and offering a suitable option for those who want to cross the next threshold.

Christians will wait till the patient rhythm of repeated conversations creates the right moment to issue a welcome invitation, such as, 'Would you like to come to our spiritual extra at the end of the gathering?'

When invitations fit the relationship, everyone can experience a fuller life, whatever their beliefs.

5. A NEGOTIATED GIFT

Appropriate to the recipient, appropriate to the giver and appropriate to the relationship: how do the three come together? This of course is where the debate begins!

How far should the gift fit the recipients? How far should it reflect the giver's traditions? If the expectations of the two are different, where should the balance lie? And how can the answer strengthen the relationship?

Empathetic dialogue

In her discussion of giving, Lee Fennell describes the negotiation that occurs inside the giver's head. The giver enters imaginatively into the life of the other and asks, 'What would the recipient most wish to receive in the context of our relationship?'

This requires insight into the other person. Perhaps a friend has little current appreciation of jazz, but unknowingly would enjoy this type of music.

Treating the person to a jazz concert would be a perceptive gift. The giver would have noticed their friend's potential gratitude, and the friend would come to see something new about herself.

Fennell calls this 'empathetic dialogue.'[14] And I would suggest that something similar happens when new Christian communities are offered to others.

Empathetic gifts

Members of the founding team prayerfully draw close to the people they seek to love, read the room with them and discuss:

- What would thrill the recipients?
- What would excite the team?
- And what would enrich the relationship?

The team's gift – or better, its gifts (plural) – start with listening, morph into activities of practical love, extend to forming community with those who come, broaden to exploring Christ with the curious, and climax with a new worshipping community, connected to the wider church, and tied to the original activity of love.

The 'dialogue' thrives when at each stage givers and recipients share empathetically one another's thinking, negotiate the next step, and rejoice together in the result.

---

[14] Lee Anne Fennell, 'Unpacking the Gift. Illiquid goods and empathetic dialogue' in Mark Osteen (ed.), *The Question of the Gift. Essays across disciplines,* Abingdon: Routledge, 2002, pp. 85-101.

6. SELF-SACRIFICE

If self-awareness is the spiritual practice for receiving first, self-surrender is the practice for giving appropriately.

Christians must start with what they have been given by God – their abilities, interests and preferences – and put them at the disposal of others. As Jesus said, only when you give your life do you find it (Matthew 16. 25).

This means shifting from self-assertion to self-donation, from putting your own desires on a pinnacle to raising up what other people want, from a consumerist attitude ('the community must be tailored to my needs') to generosity of heart ('the community exists for others'), and from hoarding God's gifts to dispersing them – from protecting the seeds to puffing the dandelion.

Here then is the essence of vivacious love. After receiving, first comes appropriate giving:

- appropriate to recipients by elevating their desires,
- appropriate to givers by sharing what you've got, and
- appropriate to the relationship by respecting the pace at which the relationship unfolds – more a bridle path, perhaps, than an expressway.

DISCUSSION

1. What have been some of the inappropriate gifts you have received?
2. Think of people you know: what would be a suitable activity of love for you to offer them?
3. Who might help you?

6. LETTING GO

We are asking about the nature of wholesome giving, using the example of giving the church to others. How can God's people become the paragon of generosity?

After receiving first and giving appropriately, the next part of the answer is releasing the gift. A gift is not a gift if you don't let go.

1. RECEIVED IN YOUR OWN WAY

If I give a toy airplane to my grandson but spend the whole afternoon holding his hand and showing him how to play with it, the present stops being a gift to him. It becomes in effect a gift to me – to relive my childhood!

But if I allow my grandson to play with the gift as he likes, I may be surprised by the result. The plane may become a car, a boat or a rocket. The boy receives the gift in his own way.

As with other aspects of giving, the Father modeled letting go when he gave his Son. Jesus did not arrive in Nazareth fully formed. He was implanted in Mary's womb, nurtured by her, raised by his parents, shaped by the local synagogue, influenced by his surroundings, and at the end of his life shaped by events.

As a gift first to the Jews, the Father released his Son into their hands. He allowed the people to receive the gift in their own way, even to the extent of putting the gift to death (Romans 8.32).

2. PASSING ON AN HEIRLOOM

Gifts slip their moorings in different ways. Chains of ownership may be placed in new hands – 'this is now yours.' Or the gift may be shared, as when a lottery winner splits her prize.

Or the gift may be more like a family heirloom. The family so values the object that it's passed down the generations. 'This necklace was given to me by my mother, who received it from hers. I would love you to have it, and then to pass it to your children.' The gift is enjoyed, while being held in trust till handed on.

The church is a bit like an heirloom. Its members reap the benefits, while guarding it for others and paying it forward.

The New Testament uses various images to describe the church, most famously the body of Christ. Might we add heirloom to the list? Though not used explicitly, heirloom is close to Paul's description of God's children as inheritors and heirs of Christ (Acts 20. 32; Romans 8. 17).

3. A PROGRESSIVE LETTING GO

When the church joins the Spirit in giving away community with Jesus, leaders will loosen their ties to the community knot by knot.

Even in the initial stages, their leadership will be gently shared. They will consult others, involve them in key decisions, and welcome offers to pitch in.

Gradually, they will hand over responsibilities to other members of the community, till eventually they pass on the leadership itself.

Otherwise, the community will not belong to those who join. As families told the founder of one new Christian community, a community is only *their* community if they can help lead it.

As leaders are progressively untethered from the community, the gift will change hands. Recipients won't end up *owning* the community, like the toy plane. Rather, as with the necklace, they will *hold it in trust*. They will treasure it on behalf of others and forward it on.

> In an area of poverty, *Sorted* has the strap line, 'A church for young people led by young people.'

Liberating the mind

Theologians from the 'global majority' have highlighted the colonization of the mind. A dominant group imposes its habit of thinking on weaker parties.

The church – with others – must plead guilty of this. It has imposed its style of Christian community on converts who lack the confidence and permission to branch out.

Rather than fully owning the faith, they live a second-hand version, the faith of those who brought the gospel. Perhaps there's nothing wrong with that at first, but it becomes unhealthy if it lasts.

Imagine the daughter being told that she can only wear the necklace with her mother's dress! Just as the daughter will want to wear the necklace with her own choice of attire, so recipients should be allowed to don the new Christian community in *their* clothes.

They must be freed to re-imagine the church, to picture a version that fits their circumstances and character. The church must be authentic to them – *but also to the Holy Spirit.*

Deferring to the Spirit

For the church is not passed on merely by those who share the gospel. It is handed on by the Spirit who works through givers and recipients.

> **"The mindset as well as leadership must be handed over"**

The Spirit is not bound by structures and traditions, even if the Spirit has had a hand in them. The Spirit is always free to innovate (John 3. 8). Or else humans would not be under the Spirit's influence; the Spirit would be under human control!

So givers of the new community must respect what the Spirit births, even if it comes as something of a surprise, even if the community is not quite what they expect.

Which means that the mindset as well as the leadership of the church must be handed over. But this won't be 'no holds barred.'

As with certain gifts, inside the box will be a set of instructions. Recipients will be given Scripture, the Christian tradition and the Holy Spirit, who will guide them in how to use the gift.

A gradual withdrawal

The time came for one leader to withdraw from her community. She did it gradually.

- She gave them plenty of warning.
- She promised to stay in touch with the new leaders.
- She stopped coming on a couple of occasions but turned up on the third.
- When she completely withdrew, she met with the new leaders from time to time. She continued to provide support while the new leaders grew in confidence.

Sometimes, when things went wrong, Paul had to intervene in his communities despite handing over the leadership. Founders of new Christian communities may need to do the same. Church structures should allow for this possibility — church leaders please note!

By drawing on these resources and support, new believers will learn how to be community with Jesus in a way that fits both them and their spiritual inheritance.

The gift will be kept within the Christian family and, we pray, become a source of delight to those who brought the gift: 'I never expected to see that!'

4. A SACRIFICIAL PROCESS

When pleading that Europeans allow the central Africa church in Cameroon to be church in a local way, Archbishop Jean Zola joked, 'Allow us to err. You yourselves have had 2000 years to err.'[15]

The risk of letting go

For givers, error can seem a big risk. Recipients may adopt beliefs and practices that seem strange. Christian themes and behavior valued by the givers may be sidelined, and new expressions of faith come to the fore.

> **"Sacrificial giving requires forgiveness"**

Those who offered the gift may be saddened because an aspect of their selves is in the gift. If parts of the gift are discarded, it may feel that a piece of themselves has been rejected.

All the time they'll also be wondering, 'Are these new Christians being faithful to Scripture?' A willingness to bear the risk of error is intrinsic to sacrificial giving, and it requires an attitude of forgiveness.

The Latin verb for 'to give,' *dono,* also means to pardon, forgive, remit. The two thoughts are connected. Both involve letting go. You let go of the gift, and you let go of your desire to avenge the wrong done to you.[16]

---

[15] Elochukwu E. Uzukwu, *A Listening Church: Autonomy and communion in African churches,* Eugene, OR: Wipf & Stock, 2006, p. 62.

[16] Robyn Horner, *Rethinking God as Gift: Marion, Derrida, and the limits of phenomenology,* New York, NY: Fordham University Press, 2001, pp. 213-214.

In letting go of the new Christian community, givers give up their right to impose a remedy if, in their view, the recipients damage the gift. No redress would be due to those who brought the gift because it is no longer theirs.

Remember the chaos at Corinth – divisions, idolatry, immorality, lawsuits between members, and that's just a start! This is what happened when Paul let go. But he took the risk.

And givers of the church must do the same. Equally, they must be on hand to help put things right if given the opportunity.

Giving involves risks, but risks are often accompanied by rewards. When you hand over your leadership, expect to see individuals flourish as they come up with ideas, assume roles they never thought themselves worthy of, and display gifts perhaps they never knew they had.

In Luke 10 Jesus shared his ministry with his disciples. When they reported back full of enthusiasm and new confidence, Jesus expressed unbridled joy. That joy can also be yours.

The heart of sacrifice

> In Britain's East Midlands, *11 Alive* emerged among families who did not connect with the existing church. They met cafe-style late Sunday mornings with bacon butties, games for the kids and newspapers for adults. At the end, there was some short, accessible worship.
>
> Every eight weeks, the community stayed for lunch and then broke into four teams. Each team prepared two acts of worship, which meant all the worship was prepared for the next eight weeks.
>
> Each team was led by a church member, but *anyone* in the community could join the team, help plan the worship and even help deliver it. An agnostic or atheist

might introduce a song, read a poem or contribute to a short talk.

Tim the minister said, 'This greatly accelerates people's journeys to faith.' When I asked, 'How many atheists and agnostics do you have in your community?' he replied: 'At present, not many. That's because most have come to faith.'

"Most have come to faith"

Releasing community with Christ is spiritual dynamite. Yet often it's not easy. Tim said that he loved preaching and leading worship. But in the past three years he had been 'up front' in the community just once. A sacrifice was involved.

Savor the joy

And that's often the case with generosity: it hurts because we let go of something that matters. So when you hand over the gift of a new Christian community, don't be surprised if it feels painful.

Equally, look for the joy. Frequently the cost in buying a present is outweighed by the giver's delight in how the gift is received.

So bask in the joy of your guests as they find a community to which they can contribute, as their ideas are taken seriously (perhaps for the first time), and as their confidence grows in their new roles.

If our prayer is that new Christian communities can lead to fuller lives, celebrate the flourishing letting go can bring.

5. SELF-RESTRAINT

If self-awareness is the spiritual practice for receiving first and self-surrender the spiritual discipline for giving appropriately, self-restraint is necessary for letting go.

Givers of the church will be a gift by making space for others to contribute. They will have big ears and little mouths.[17]

> **"Big ears and little mouths"**

Each stage of the initiative will be co-created with those involved – the initial listening, developing an activity of love, forging community with participants, sharing the gospel, and forming a new worshipping community with those who respond.

Sharing their leadership will require self-restraint by the founding team as members listen to the community,

---

[17] This image is drawn from Elochukwu Uzukwu, *A Listening Church: Autonomy and communion in African churches,* Eugene, OR: Wipf and Stock, 2006 (1996), pp. 127-128.

surrender some of their cherished ideas, fan into flame the ideas of others, and take the risk that things will go drastically wrong.

Don't despair if they do! Remember Corinth. Paul had his problems, but his heart was also warmed by the fruits of his new communities.

Writing to the Philippian church he could say, 'I thank my God every time I remember you. In all my prayers for all of you, I always pray with joy' (Philippians 1. 3-4).

From my home to your home

Maybe the new community's story will look like this:

- *'Welcome to my home.'* As the founding team, you've taken the first step, if only to listen. So it's your initiative to start with. But quickly this becomes...

- *'Welcome to our home.'* You and those you love work together to create a joint initiative – a community *with*, not a community for.

- *'Welcome to your home.'* You nurture new leaders and progressively hand over the community to them.

- *'Welcome to God's home.'* As the community becomes authentic to its members, to the Christian family and to the Spirit working unpredictably in its midst, it becomes a home fit for Jesus.

Sabotaging power

This subverts power-hungry approaches to mission. Community in Christ is given not in the spirit of control or self-aggrandizement, nor by keeping recipients in a place of dependency.

It is offered as a gift of the Spirit, who releases it progressively into recipients' hands. As power is transferred from givers to receivers, the latter are enabled to bloom.

We can revel in their vibrant lives like we relish the spring. Yet it is the autumn leaves that remind us how beautiful letting go can be.

DISCUSSION

1. What are your experiences (in any context) of good and bad delegation?

2. What principles should govern the handing over of leadership? Can you think of examples from Scripture or the church?

3. How could potential leaders be nurtured in a new Christian community?

7. ACCEPTING THE GIFT

Some people worry that giving away new Christian communities will fragment the church. Congregations will multiply, but they will be lonely islands rather than forming an ecclesiastical archipelago.

Worse, these islands will be culturally segregated. Each new community will gather the likeminded. Distinctiveness will spell difference. Difference will erect barriers to other Christian groups.

Communities will stand apart from, become suspicious of, or even be hostile to one another. Church fragments will lacerate the body with their serrated edges of fancied superiority.

Here then is the tension: a new Christian community must fit the recipients; it must meet at a time and place, with a style and an agenda that are accessible. Equally, it must hold hands with congregations with whom it may sharply disagree. Can a new community do both?

1. FORMING COMMUNITY

The answer makes the next dimension of giving especially important. After receiving first, giving appropriately, and letting go comes accepting the gift. A gift must be received.

And accepting the gift is the moment when giving achieves its social purpose – to create community. Giving builds relationships, and this happens most critically when the gift is received.

Accepting the gift, accepting the giver

Givers offer part of themselves in their gifts. So when recipients accept a gift the giver is accepted too, which strengthens the connection – the community – between them.

Offering the gift is not enough in itself. What is decisive is the recipient's response. If the gift is accepted the relationship is deepened. The recipient feels grateful and the giver relishes the gratitude. Both are drawn closer to each other.

Any hint of rejection, however, is a blow. The giver feels rejected, the recipient may feel resentful or embarrassed, and there's tension between the two.

Unseen communities

Strikingly, many gifts do something more. They draw you into a *larger* community, a community of people who enjoy the same gift. Even though the community may go unnoticed, when you accept the gift you enter that community.

For instance, a gift of swimming lessons connects the child to others in the same class. The gift of a pair of fashionable shoes connects the recipient to people who appreciate that style of footwear.

True, these fashion aficionados will not all know each other. So they are not a *visible* community. But if a community is a group with certain attitudes and interests in common, they are an *implicit* community, a crowd you fall in with but never meet.

These communities exist whether or not you accept the gift. *Receiving* the gift is what connects you to them.

So when you accept the gift, you not only cement your ties to the giver, you tacitly accept the community that accompanies the gift.

The community of disciples

And that's especially true of the church. The gift of a new Christian community is more than the community itself. It is the gift of the whole communion of saints, of which the community is but a tiny part. It is only when you receive the particular community that you become part of this wider community.

In the gospels, Jesus initially preached and healed on his own. As some people accepted him, one by one a community of disciples emerged.

Later Jesus sent these disciples in pairs to the surrounding villages and towns as representatives of him and, by implication, the whole community (Luke 10). Welcoming each pair meant accepting Jesus and his community.

That continues today. When we publicly accept Jesus in baptism, we join all others who have received him (Mark 3. 34).

Of course, as in my shoes example, we won't be aware of all

the other congregations, let alone know them. Even so, invisible though it is, we shall belong to something bigger and real.

2. A COMMUNITY OF CONNECTIONS

The invisible church has pockets of visibility. These windows are the Christian communities we see across the world, tied together in a lattice of networks.

Starting with the apostles and repeated through history, Christian communities have multiplied as Jesus has been gratefully received, recipients have gathered around him in a new community, and one gathering has connected to another.

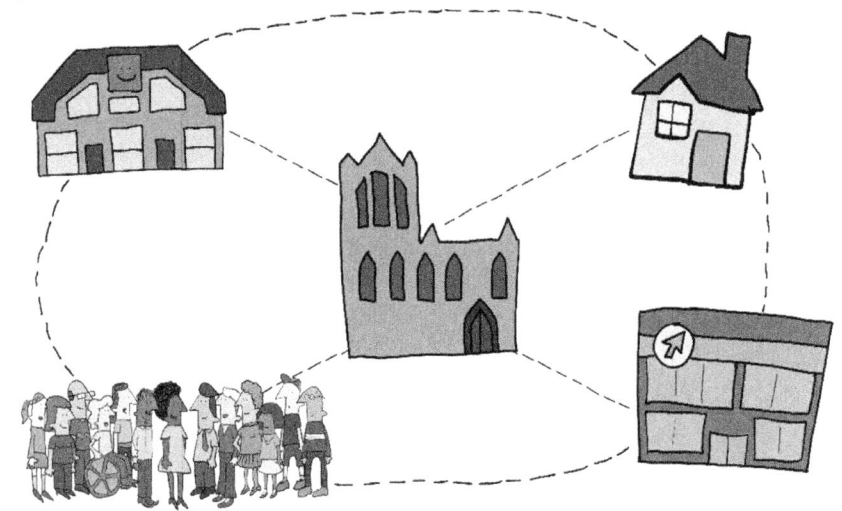

Like a wheel

Increasingly today these new communities are given by a local congregation and retain links with it. Each new community, we pray, will spawn further gatherings (congregations in effect), which at their best will incubate further Christian communities.

Think of a wheel. At the hub is the parent congregation. Around the rim are its children, which are connected to the hub by the wheel's spokes and to each other by the rim. In time, some children may become hubs with their own offspring.

When a wheel spins, it looks as if the spokes are merging together, although in reality they are distinct. And that's the ideal. Each community keeps its specific identity, but relationships with other congregations crisscross in a fluid web.

> **"Connecting up is the expressway to sustainability"**

Connect! Connect!

One woman accepted Jesus through a *Knit and Natter* community. She became friends with someone who attended the parent church. So she started going too.

She couldn't believe that she was now 'at church' three times a week – once at *Knit and Natter* and twice through the parent congregation.

Connecting with the wider church enriched her spiritual life. It also opened routes to an alternative congregational home were *Knit and Natter* to run its course.

Connecting up is the highway to sustainability.

3. JOINED-UP CHURCH

Connecting up really matters – for these reasons:

- **It builds resilience.** As I've said, if a new community comes to the end of its natural life, members will know Christians from another congregation who can help them find a new spiritual home.

- **It grows disciples.** New Christians are freed from the parish of their minds. They become aware of theological, liturgical, missional and organizational insights from other parts of the church.

- **It aids discernment.** Christian communities need not navigate the truth on their own. They can avoid error through the wisdom of fellow travelers. 'It takes the whole church to reveal the whole Christ.' At the same time...

- **It keeps things simple.** Believers can avoid drowning in a sea of theological argument and spiritual options. Their local church and its denomination or network will have preselected essential beliefs and practices from the vast menu in the global church. 'This is what we believe and do.' So new congregations needn't exhaust themselves by choosing at every turn and constantly reinventing the wheel. They can just take the prescription.

- **It enriches the whole.** Congregations can share their gifts with each other. Not least, wealthier congregations can support poorer ones, a priority for New Testament believers.

- **It spreads innovation.** Congregations can be seedbeds of novelty. They can adapt or combine ideas from a variety of sources to create and test something new. When an experiment proves fruitful, church networks will broadcast the innovation.

- **It facilitates mission.** Some undertakings are too big for a single congregation. Christian communities can combine for mission at local, regional, national and international levels.

4. A NEW TESTAMENT MODEL

If a new Christian community comes in a package of the whole church, how can recipients accept the wider body so that they benefit from it?

In my swimming lessons example, this is the equivalent of a father asking, 'How can my daughter get to know others in the class?'

Perhaps he offers to share lifts with families nearby. The child receives the gift (she travels to the class) in a way that creates opportunities to make friends (a couple of fellow swimmers journey with her).

So with recipients of a new Christian community. They must be enabled to accept not a solo community but joined-up church – a community that is friends with the church at large.

Not many people realize this, but the first Christians showed how. They met in culturally distinct groups, the house churches. These groups also came together from time to time. Bespoke gatherings combined in generic assemblies.

Tailor-made congregations

House churches were culturally diverse. They were scattered across cities like Jerusalem, Antioch and Corinth, and seem to have drawn people from the neighborhood.[18]

Ancient cities were ethnically and socially segmented, as they are today. Different neighborhoods had different flavors. And these differences were reflected in the Jewish synagogues, which catered for distinct cultural groups (Acts 6. 9).

As Jews, the first Christians would have been influenced by the synagogues they'd grown up with. So they would have assumed that their churches, too, would vary from social niche to niche.

Don't be confused by the presence of slaves and masters in the same gathering (Ephesians 6. 5-9; James 2. 1-4). In our terms these gatherings were socially very diverse, but in the first century they belonged to the same household. They were part of the same affiliative niche out which the house church grew.

---

[18] Richard Last, 'The neighbourhood (*vicus*) of the Corinthian *ekklesia*: beyond family-based descriptions of the first urban Christ-based believers', *Journal for the Study of the New Testament*, 38 (4), 2016, p. 417.

Heterogeneous assemblies

Are niche congregations a red flag for you, at odds with St Paul's vision of a church without ethnic, social and other divides (Galatians 3. 28)?

If so, you can pull the flag down. When a first-century believer accepted community with Christ, they didn't join one of these niche churches alone. They came into a much larger community.

> **"Niche churches gathered in city-wide assemblies"**

First, they intermingled with other bespoke churches in a periodic city-wide assembly. In Jerusalem, for example, believers broke bread in people's homes, but also came together 'every day' in the temple courts (Acts 2. 46).

Antioch seems to have had the same pattern. Galatians 2. 11-14 assumes that a number of house churches existed.[19] But the confrontation between Paul and Peter took place 'in front of them all' (Galatians, 2. 14). All the house churches were in one gathering.

In 1 Corinthians 14. 23 Paul refers to the 'whole church' coming together. Again, there seems to have been niche churches in people's homes and city-wide gatherings that mixed these churches up.

---

[19] Roger W. Gehring, *House Church and Mission: The importance of household structure in early Christianity*, Peabody, MA: Hendrickson, 2004, p. 112.

A holy internet

Secondly, new Christian were drawn into an even larger community. When they accepted life with Jesus, the gift came in three tiers: the neighborhood church, the city-wide assembly, and connections to believers in other cities.

There was a 'holy internet' as believers with strict Jewish practices came from Jerusalem to Antioch, people carried letters from one place to another, financial gifts were collected from different cities and taken to believers in need, and itinerant preachers and prophets travelled between Christian communities.[20]

House churches were not isolated planets but orbited around a city-wide gathering, which in turn was connected to an ecclesiastical Milky Way.

Both/and

So here's how New Testament Christians addressed the danger of a segregated church, of culturally distinct churches developing separately.

When someone accepted community with Christ, they were drawn into a wider gathering that spanned social divides. They belonged to a both/and church that held together:

- neighborhood churches and city-wide assemblies,
- social similarity and diversity,
- small meetings and larger ones,
- the safety of a known group and the challenge of people with different outlooks,

---

[20] Michael B. Thompson, 'The holy internet: communication between churches in the first Christian generation' in Richard Bauckham (ed.), *The Gospels for All Christians: Rethinking the gospel audiences,* Grand Rapids, MI: Eerdmans, 1998.

- intimacy with looser relationships, and
- the church in a particular city with the church elsewhere.

This was far from easy, as the rows in Corinth illustrate, but the first Christians seem to have made it a priority.

5. CONNECTING UP TODAY

In our very different world, the same basic pattern applies. New Christian communities should connect to their local church or congregation, which should have ties to the church at large.

These bonds should be so strong that there can be no doubt: when you accept the new community you accept the whole church.

In practice this means nailing down pathways from each new community to the wider body.

Here are eight ideas:

- **'Huddles' between founding teams and church leaders.** This is vital not just for accountability, but to lay the foundations of further ties with the parent church.

  > Christ Church has several outreach activities such as *Cake and Create* and a group for recent immigrants. A minister draws the leaders together from time to time to plan, learn from each other, receive input, pray, and inspire one another. They are forming the habit of connecting, which they can pass on to their new communities.

- **Sharing the weekly notice sheet** from as early a stage as possible. Print it off and scatter around copies. It will remind your community that it's part of something bigger. Maybe the parent congregation is forming a choir for the carol service or needs help in the office. Someone spots this and volunteers. He starts feeling he belongs to the church way before calling himself a churchgoer.

- **Interest groups** can build bridges between the new community and the existing congregation. What about an ecology group, a community coffee morning, a reading group, a running group? Might someone in the new community help start it?

- **Social events** can draw long-standing and new Christians together. You don't have to wait for a community to become a *Christian* community. Invite members to a 'social' now!

- **Combined worship events,** such as a carol service, an Easter celebration, a pet service, or a monthly Holy Communion.

- **A Christian festival, conference or inter-church prayer retreat** can speed journeys to Christ, deepen new-found faith, and introduce the wider church.

- **Invitations to join your giving scheme.** Not to be done too quickly! Nor to be forgotten. Generosity is a serious Christian practice.

- **Church governance.** At the right time, ask if your new community is properly represented in your church's structures.

6. WELCOME

If self-awareness, self-surrender and self-restraint support the first three aspects of generosity, here is a fourth brick with which to build a spirituality of giving: receiving the whole church requires the spiritual habit of welcome.

Newcomers must welcome the greater church, but just as important, *the greater church must welcome the newcomers.*

The whole body must extend a welcome to each new Christian community however different. It must stand ready to receive what the community has to offer, however unexpected these gifts may first appear.

Of course, like a parent educating a child, the wider church will share its wisdom about what is an appropriate return gift (what would honor the church's head). But this will always be done with an inviting smile.

And the smile will broaden as the universal church receives fresh insights into the gospel, new ways of expressing the faith in worship and mission, and new resources of time, talents and treasure.

Being accepted by the greater church will help new communities to feel at home. Feeling welcomed will increase their security and gratitude. And feeling more confident and thankful will help them step with greater assurance into the wider church, bringing ever larger gifts with them.

So here's the prize: through the grace of welcome, the whole church will accept the new Christian community while the new community will embrace the bigger church.

New Christians will join not just a fragment of the church. Mutual welcome will join the fragments up.

DISCUSSION

1. What do you find attractive and unattractive about the wider church?

2. How do you and your local congregation connect to the church at large?

3. What stepping stones would lead new Christians into the whole body of Christ?

8. GIVING BACK

Giving builds relationships. That's one of its purposes. But it only does this well if giving is reciprocal. The giver feels used if the recipient never gives back, while recipients may feel embarrassed or inadequate if they cannot return a gift.

Were a friend to give you a birthday present, it wouldn't feel right not to give a present back at some stage.

However, we feel uncomfortable with this sense of obligation. So we fool ourselves by wrapping our sense of duty in a story of altruism. 'I am being generous.' 'I am being kind.'

Yet no matter how well concealed, the obligation to give back remains hidden within the gift. 'I want to give' is tinged with 'I ought.'

> **"We disguise duty in wrapping paper of altruism"**

Don't be too disillusioned, though. It's not either/or – either duty or altruism. At its best, return giving is both/and – both duty and altruism.

I feel obliged to be altruistic. But when I imagine the pleasure that results, giving becomes an alchemy. It turns duty into gilded joy.

1. LOOK AT JESUS

The to-and-fro of giving was modeled by Jesus. He first received the gift of his Jewish inheritance; he attended a Temple workshop, for example (Luke 2. 41-52).

Then in his public ministry he gave back to his inheritance. In Matthew 5, for instance, he repeated six times, 'You have heard it said, but I say to you.'

He was not correcting the Old Testament law, but correcting what the people had been taught about the law. By offering new insights, he gave his fellow Jews the gift of renewing their heritage.

2. EXPRESSING GRATITUDE

The most obvious giving back is gratitude – hence the word 'thanks*giving*'. Perhaps you've never thought of gratitude as a gift. But when you say 'Thank you' (and mean it!) you delight the giver. (And anything that brings joy is potentially a gift.)

But here's the rub: you do have to mean it. Otherwise, your thanks are hollow. And there is enough emptiness in the world already.

In debt to the church

New Christian communities, please note this: you have been offered communal life with Jesus by members of the church.

These members have been spiritually nurtured by the church. Their characters and outlooks have been formed by centuries of Christian learning and wisdom.

As they have shared the gospel, they have been prayed for and sometimes paid for by the wider church. Some of their sacrifices for you were inspired by life within the church at large.

In human terms, your debt to the church is a mountain. And so the most suitable gift you can first offer back is gratitude – not just thanks to those who brought you the gift, but thanks to the wider church who made the gift possible.

An example

Imagine leaders of a new community are keen to forge links with the parent congregation. So they suggest that the community joins the congregation in their Easter celebration.

Members of the community arrive in plenty of time, find a pew, look at the backs of worshipers in front of them, go to the church hall for refreshments afterwards, huddle in a circle, and then leave having spoken to hardly anyone else.

Will they come again?....

So much for connecting up!

But here's another scenario. The leaders have a word with organizers of the coffee rota. They suggest their community serves refreshments after the service.

Now the community is at the center of the action! People talk to its members as they serve, learn something about the new Christian community, and express *their* thanks.

No longer is the congregation suspicious of the new community ('When are we going to see them in church?'). Rather they have noticed the community, appreciated it, and begun to make it feel part of the whole.

What's happened? The community has expressed its thanks visibly to the parent congregation. And this in turn has softened the hearts of the congregation. Instead of feeling on the edge, the community has been welcomed in.

Converting the congregation

Often leaders of new Christian communities complain that the parent congregation is indifferent, sometimes even hostile to the new community. The congregation is not welcoming the community as it ought.

They assume that giving should be from the hub to the rim, from the parent congregation to the new community on the church's edge.

> "Not from hub to rim, but from rim to the hub"

But this puts the shoe on the wrong foot. The congregation has already offered a gift, the gift of the new community. The next move is for the community to give a 'thank you' in return.

Giving should be from the rim to the hub. That is the lodestar for connecting up.

Otherwise the community would be like someone who allows everyone else to buy the drinks, but never does so himself.

If the relationship is to be healthy, the new community cannot always be at the receiving end of generosity. There has to be a giving back. Return generosity opens the door to a deeper relationship.

And it is the founding team's responsibility to start the ball rolling. *It* must lay pathways along which the community's thanks can travel.

After all, the team knows both the parent congregation and the new community. *It* is best placed to bring the two together in mutual generosity. If the team doesn't do it, who will?

3. PASSING ON

Here is another way that new communities can express their gratitude. They owe much to Christians in earlier centuries who contributed to the church and passed it on. Without these previous generations, the new community would not exist.

Thanking the past

The trouble is that Christians today have no direct way of thanking their spiritual forebears. They are like an adult who comes to appreciate a school teacher but cannot directly thank him.

Instead, she may express her gratitude by diligently passing on her own skill or knowledge to others. 'What you did for me,' she thinks, 'I'll do for other people.'

Were she to give flowers to a neighbor as her 'thank you', her random response would raise startled eyebrows. Instead, she does something the teacher would value and this becomes her return gift.

Likewise, recipients of the church can thank earlier generations by passing on to other people their own experience of the tradition, the essence of which is gathering around Jesus. 'Just as you shared community with Christ with others, we too will pass the gift on.'

Remaining a gift

Lewis Hyde points out, 'A gift that cannot move loses its gift properties.'[21] The object becomes a possession to be consumed by its owner. Only if the object is viewed as something to be passed on does it retain its gift status.

A present of biscuits stays a gift if you share it with friends. But it becomes a possession if you consume it on your own.

Jesus is always a gift. He is always there for others. As his body, the church too must remain a gift.

The church can do this in many ways as I have said, but supremely in the gift of itself, the very heart of its life, which is community with Jesus.

Handing on communal life with Christ saves the community from being possessed by its members. Instead, it becomes a return gift to Christians in previous ages (as well as a first gift to others today). When recipients in their turn pass the gift on, God's people become a perpetual gift.

The church is not like perishable goods that cannot be continuously handed over; once eaten, they are no longer

---

[21] Lewis Hyde, *The Gift. How the Creative Spirit Transforms the World*, Edinburgh: Canongate, 2012, p. 8.

available. It is more like a tweet or music file. It can be forwarded without leaving the hands of the giver.

> **"The body of Christ becomes the self-multiplication of Christ"**

The gift is not depleted when it's given, though of course the file can be deleted, just as congregations can die. The gift spreads.

As a result, the body of Christ becomes the self-multiplication of Christ. Worth thinking about?

4. GIVING SOMETHING NEW

Return gifts are not the same as the original gift. Imagine my brother and I always gave each other identical birthday presents! Giving works because the first gift and the return gift are different.

This *has* to be the case because, you'll remember, something of the giver is in the gift – their choice of gift, what they think is appropriate and so on. The gift says something about the giver as well as the recipient. Gifts must vary because givers vary, as do recipients.

Just as contributions to a conversation are different ('copycat' would kill it), so with gifts in general. They bring something new to the conversation of life. After the Easter service, new people were behind the hatch.

Classic cars

The parent congregation and church at large, therefore, must expect return gifts that come as a surprise:

- New ways of worship – new songs and liturgies, for example.

- New insights into the gospel.

- New ways of organizing a Christian community.

- New forms of mission.

> Adam, for example, loves classic cars. He has gathered a group of fellow car enthusiasts who meet regularly to show off their cars in the summer and to watch car films during winter.
>
> He has begun to give them a written 'Thought for the day' as they leave, based around their love of cars. 'What do we use to eradicate rust?' for example. 'What might remove some of the spiritual rust in our lives?'
>
> On one occasion, he invited the group to bring car parts that were 'beautifully and wonderfully made.' This led to a discussion about our beautiful and wonderful world, and how it came to exist.
>
> What Adam is beginning to do is to co-create a Christian spirituality that draws from the everyday life of classic cars, just as Jesus drew from his everyday world of agriculture.

Patchwork spirituality

Now imagine a future in which thousands of new Christian communities were developing 'local theologies' like this, and that they were sharing their insights as gifts back to the universal church. New ideas and practices would zigzag across the ecclesial terrain.

The big win would be a church immersed in the crevices of everyday experience, attentive to the hills and valleys of life, and with an echoing storehouse of stories that vibrate in people's hearts.

The existing church, therefore, should not defend itself against unexpected gifts, however unusual, from its new congregations. Instead, it should pray that through these gifts:

- the tradition will be broadened by innovation while novelties are deepened by tradition,

- the old will dodge irrelevance while the new sidesteps transience,

- smaller communities will introduce people to Jesus while the larger church gives believers a fuller picture,

- newcomers will be welcomed while old timers are esteemed.

5. CONVERTING THE CHURCH

Christians widely assume that the Spirit uses the church to convert others. But voices in the majority world have insisted that the Spirit can also work through new believers to convert the *church*.

Non-believers come to faith, and then they help the church become more faithful itself. Receivers of the church are converted to Jesus; next they help the original givers to see a fuller Jesus.

This second conversion is made possible by return giving. Among gifts back to the wider body are offerings that enable it to become more true to its head.

The four marks

I have suggested three examples.

- Showing gratitude explicitly to the parent congregation can help the latter become more welcoming to the new community. As old and new draw together, they will show more fully the church's oneness.

- Handing on the community to others is an appropriate return gift to former generations who passed on the church themselves. The church will be more faithful to the apostles, for whom handing on the church was a priority. It will become more apostolic.

- Giving back to the church new insights into the gospel will broaden the church's horizons. The church will become more diverse in its membership, its thinking, and its practices. It will become more catholic.

As the church becomes more faithful to Jesus in these ways, more of Christ's holiness (what makes him unique) will rub off on the church.

The church will be more obviously one, holy, catholic and apostolic, the marks we affirm in the Nicene creed.

6. A SPIRITUAL DISCIPLINE

What spiritual habits will foster these return gifts to the church? Thanksgiving is clearly one:

- To the parent congregation for supporting the founders of the new Christian community.
- To previous generations who passed on the church.
- To the new community, whose gospel innovations burst the banks of the tradition.
- And most of all to God, the dawn of it all.

DISCUSSION

1. How big a part should obligation play in return giving?
2. How can new Christian communities be encouraged to thank their parent congregation?
3. In what ways might these new communities be surprising gifts to the wider church?

9. TRANSFORMATION

Healthy giving, I suggest, involves receiving first, giving appropriately, letting go, accepting the gift, giving back, and – in this chapter – transformation.

Each cycle of giving spins around these ingredients, but the cycles entwine so that the elements crisscross each other.

In the case of two friends for example, one may be preparing a surprise birthday party, while the other sends a return gift – 'Thank you for babysitting last week.' The birthday party is part of one cycle of giving, 'thank you for babysitting' another. The two cycles overlap.

When these giving cycles swirl around the church and bubble out to the surrounding world, God's people become a more welcome gift.

1. TRANSFORMED GIVERS

Jesus experienced a change when he gave himself to the world. This was not a change in his eternal character of love, total knowledge and so on. What was new was the Son of God's experience of human life, death and resurrection.

Like Jesus, givers in general are transformed – perhaps imperceptibly – by the process of giving. Their flow of life may be enhanced by anticipating the joy their gift will bring, by the satisfaction of making or choosing the present, or by feeling better about themselves because they have done the right thing.

New identity, new life

Similarly, givers of new Christian communities find their lives are transformed. Maybe they see the church in a new way, as a gift not a possession.

This brings a change in their involvement. The parent congregation re-arranges its life around generosity to people outside, as do founders of the new community. Identities are re-shaped.

> For example, in 2010 Christ Church, in England's West Midlands, felt that it was too inward looking. So it re-focused on giving to people beyond the church.
>
> Members started a walking group, coffee mornings for patients of a medical practice, a monthly discussion for older people, a thriving youth group and more.
>
> In 2010, the church was serving 250 people. Five years later, the number had doubled to 500!

Dying to live

The core of giving, most poignantly demonstrated on the cross, is dying to self and coming alive to others. Givers surrender their preferences to those of the recipients.

Founders of new Christian communities may let certain commitments die to free up time for the people they are called to.

In particular, they may die to their expectations of what worship in their new community will be like. This is not dying to the tradition itself, but to how it will be expressed. They give space for the Spirit to birth something new.

The parent congregation as a whole may experience several 'deaths', such as:

- The departure of the team to start a new community.
- The closing of a church activity to unlock resources for mission.
- The splintering of a weekly congregation into communities for mission that come together just once a month.

Yet these 'deaths' need not be the last word. The congregation may partially fragment as it multiplies, but the Spirit can stitch the fragments together in a more contemporary fabric.

When the parent congregation is enriched by a new community, disintegration (however small) is followed by reintegration, a kind of death by fresh kinds of life.

2. TRANSFORMED RECIPIENTS

Receivers of the Christian community are changed because a fresh take is added to their days. Perhaps they start attending a grief group, and then a 'spiritual extra' alongside it.

New dimensions

At an inter-generational *Messy Church* in south London, parents and children absorbed Christian stories and songs. They talked about the stories and sang the songs at home.

This impacted their lives in small but significant ways. One child didn't like his mother saying 'God' or 'Jesus' in a disrespectful way.[22] The gift had switched on a spiritual light bulb.

Apprentices

Or imagine a plumbing specialist who spots an ability in his niece, draws it to her attention, helps nurture it, and makes her his apprentice.

As the apprentice develops her talent, she is gradually transformed from a stumbling to a proficient plumber.

Then she takes on an apprentice herself. She has become like her uncle both in his plumbing skills and in his desire to pass those skills on.

A similar change happens to recipients of a new Christian community. They become like the founders of the community, who hand on to them the 'skill' of Christ-like generosity.

3. TRANSFORMED SOCIETY

Not only are givers and receivers transformed, but also the world around them. This partly happens through the

---

[22] Clare Watkins and Bridget Shepherd, 'The challenge of "Fresh Expressions" to ecclesiology. Reflections from the practice of messy church', *Ecclesial Practices,* 1 (2014), p. 104.

dynamics of thanks.

Robert Roberts argues that being grateful can reduce the anger, resentment, envy, and bitterness that threaten healthy relationships. Gratitude is an antidote to negative emotions. It re-energizes healthy feelings, which neutralizes the poison.[23]

> "Gratitude is an antidote to negative emotions"

Not least, thankfulness trains the brain to seed gratitude into other relationships. Feeling better about life in one context, the person becomes more disposed to be grateful in another. Gratitude here sings songs of thanks there.

Offering new Christian communities is a great way to amplify this music of gratefulness.

- People are embraced by a community with giving at its heart.
- Others' generosity makes them more thankful.
- Gratitude boosts their sense of wellbeing.
- Feeling good boosts their self-esteem.
- Inner strength helps them be more generous themselves.
- Aromatic waves of kingdom giving, thankfulness and further generosity are released into society.

---

[23] Roberts C. Roberts., "The Blessings of Gratitude. A Conceptual Analysis" in Robert A. Emmons and Michael E. McCullough (eds), *The Psychology of Gratitude*, Oxford: OUP, 2004, p. 59.

Organized love

Sometimes we have a rather weak notion of love. We reduce it to happy one-to-one chats. But love is much more than this. Often love has to be organized.

Think of a family: getting the children to school, fixing the evening meal, planning the holidays, arranging a birthday party and so much more. All these are activities of love, but they have to be orchestrated.

Now, many single parents do this on their own brilliantly. But how much easier – and more fun – when love is planned with other people.

Starting a new Christian community is an example of organized love. You have to map out what you're going to do, find a place to meet and so on.

When the community's spiritual life blossoms, one of the fruits will be the capacity and desire to arrange further activities of love.

> For example, two couples hosted a community breakfast one Sunday a month for their immediate neighborhood.
>
> As people crammed into the small house, others began to start ice cream parties in the summer, chocolate parties in the winter, gatherings in the pub, a parent-and-toddler group, and Christian spirituality sessions.
>
> Organized love pumped through the neighborhood and sprinkled lives with joy.

More to give

Here is the transformational potential of giving away new Christian communities. They bring to God's people:

- More volunteers.
- More charitable activities and organizations.
- More capacity to campaign on social and environmental issues.
- More money to invest in pastoral care and reconciliation.
- More gifts in music, art and poetry to share with others.

The church has a larger basket from which to feed the world.

4. TELLING STORIES

As we build a spirituality of giving, a spiritual practice to support the transformational aspect of generosity is storytelling. Stories are so part of life (think of gossip!) that we take them for granted.

But good stories are gifts, and like all gifts they involve:

- *Receiving first.* You receive other people by paying attention to them so that your story connects with them.

- *Giving appropriately.* The story must fit the other person, be true to you, and fit the particular stage of the conversation.

- *Letting go.* You allow hearers to accept the story in their own way.

- *Receiving.* Hearers show that they have heard and understood the story.

- *Giving back.* They respond with a comment or perhaps another story.

- *Transformation.* You are all changed in a small way; maybe you laugh together.

Stories become a *spiritual* practice when Christians pepper anecdotes that accompany generosity with a particular type of story.

These gifts will show concern for the hearer, respect people who are part of the story, reveal something of the teller's spiritual life, and contribute to a larger narrative about God.

As hearers engage with the stories, they may be changed by receiving new information, seeing an issue in a fresh light, or experiencing a change in their emotions.

These stories become vehicles for the Spirit to support the back-and-forth giving that births a new community. The Spirit's mini stories of kindness can love people into God's mega story of graciousness.

DISCUSSION

1. From your life in the church, what are your favorite examples of organized love?

2. Can you think of lives that have been changed through these activities?

3. If Jesus said you could do anything you want, what kind of organized love would you choose to be involved with?

4. What is the closest to this around you, and might you talk to someone about it?

10. BEYOND HOSPITALITY

It is common today to describe the church's mission as hospitality. By extending hospitality to people outside the church, newcomers are welcomed into the hospitality of God.

When offering new Christian communities, the emphasis is on inviting people to the feast of heaven, giving them a warm welcome, and making them feel at home. Time and again, food is on the menu!

1. HAVE WE OVER EMPHASIZED HOSPITALITY?

When a team begins to offer communion with Jesus, the initiative will be theirs. They will invite others to join in by listening to them and discovering with them what would be an appropriate gift.

As team members do this, they will make the invitation attractive through their joyful welcome and by making people feel at ease in their company.

Hospitality is a good way to frame the team's generosity at this stage. The team is opening its arms to others.

But hospitality is not a good description of what happens next. Giving away new Christian communities involves generosity that far outstrips hospitality.

Surpassing hospitality

One problem with hospitality is that guests have to fit in with the host's expectations. If you are invited to stay in someone's home, the home is not a gift to be received however you want. You can't prescribe what food is served, change the rules of the household, or go about redecorating the rooms.

As Robyn Horner points out, hospitality works precisely because the gift is limited. By dictating the terms, hosts ring fence their generosity.[24]

If hospitality is the extent of the church's giving, generosity will become paternalistic. God's people will assume they know best, set the conditions, and keep control.

---

[24] Robyn Horner, *Rethinking God as Gift: Marion, Derrida, and the Limits of Phenomenology,* New York, NY: Fordham University Press, 2001, p. 12.

They'll say in effect, 'We are inviting you to what *we've* created.' They'll consult recipients, but the final decision will be in the givers' hands. The gift will not be released. Nor will recipients be encouraged to receive it in *their* own way.

Firm boundaries may be inevitable at the start. But when the community begins to take shape, the shutters must be opened so that a bigger view of giving comes into sight.

Members shouldn't feel that the leaders are patronizingly doing things *for* them or *to* them. It should be community *with*, not community *for*.

Passing on the leadership of the new community – 'What we've created is now yours' – is generosity that far exceeds hospitality.

- First, you share your decision-making with the community.
- Then you mentor people who might become leaders.
- Next you bring them into the leadership team.
- Later, you hand your leadership over to them but continue to provide support.
- In time, you progressively reduce your support.

This transfer of power sweeps away the constraints of hospitality and brings perhaps a surprise at the end. When you give away the community completely, *you* become the guest!

Sharing beyond hospitality

Here's another problem. When you restrict generosity to hospitality you limit the opportunity for others to contribute.

Often leaders think they are being generous when the core team provides the food at the community's main event. And again, this may be appropriate at the beginning.

But imagine that after a while not just the leaders, but members bring and share the food. Here's an opportunity for people to reveal unexpected preferences and cooking talents.

> One community in an area of poverty asked *everyone* to contribute, however poor. If they couldn't afford to bring food, they brought their time and helped to set up and clear away. This boosted people's self-esteem. Everyone had something to share.

> Remember *11 Alive* in Chapter 6? Atheists and agnostics were invited to help prepare a short act of worship and contribute to it. They might say a prayer, introduce a song or read a poem. It greatly accelerated their journeys to faith.

These examples outshine our normal understanding of hospitality. Community members stop being guests and become participants. They are not just receivers, they are givers. Outsiders become insiders.

Showing a fuller Jesus

Maybe you are praying that your community will become a full expression of Christ's body. In which case, just as gestures express the thoughts in a person's head, the community must express the church's head. So what is your community saying about Jesus?

This is a third problem with hospitality. It provides too thin a picture of Christ. By welcoming people as guests, it unwittingly implies that Jesus invites them to be guests of his family.

Now once again that may be appropriate to start with. Being a guest enables you to see the community in action and decide whether you want to be more involved.

But it cannot be the whole story. The gift Jesus offers is not to be guests of God's family. It's to become *members* of it – to become children of the heavenly Father and siblings of Christ.

Hospitality is a far cry from the language of adoption in the New Testament. To adopt someone is a huge act of generosity, much more than inviting them to be a guest.

You might say, 'All this is true, Mike, but only if you have a limited view of hospitality. Our view of hospitality is much bigger than what you've described. It includes letting the new community go, inviting members to contribute, and modeling Christ's invitation to belong.'

But if that's your view of hospitality, it is not what most people understand by the term. It sounds more like unreserved generosity. And that's my point. You may start with hospitality, but as you expand your welcome, your kindness will flood the limits of hospitality and spill into unstinting generosity.

Generosity is a much better description of the church's mission because it includes hospitality but goes beyond it. It reaches toward the unlimited giving of Christ.

So if your community is to demonstrate God's expansive giving, it must strain beyond *hospitality*. It must share in God's full-throated *generosity*.

2. A WELCOME GIFT?

This brings us back to the question at the start of the book. If Christian generosity involves offering the church, can

God's people be a gift anyone would want to receive? Given its manifold shortcomings, can the church be a welcome gift?

I would suggest that full-blooded giving is fundamental to the answer. Offering God's people ethically can help rewire the church's structures and practices. As the church gives its self to others, its own life will be reformed.

Receiving first

This includes careful listening, not least to painful criticisms of the church. Rebukes can move God's people to repentance, renewal, and to sacrificial service that others recognize as reparation.

The core team might ask, 'Given your disgust at spiritual abuse in the church, can you help us to take safeguarding seriously?' The church is provoked to make itself a more acceptable gift.

Appropriate giving

Giving the church appropriately invites God's people to consider what kind of gift they might be. What form of communal life in Jesus would be received with delighted thanks?

It also invites the church to ask, 'What is a suitable gift for *us* to offer?' God's people will look at themselves through the prism of generosity. 'What interests, resources and contacts do we have that can make us a gift?'

Appropriate giving includes, too, what is proper to both sides' investment in the relationship, to how much the relationship means to them.

So before offering the heart of their life, community with Christ, God's people will ask whether this is a fitting gift at that stage.

Have they poured out enough love to potential recipients, and has this love been sufficiently reciprocated for such an offer to be suitable?

Sensitive giving, with recipients uppermost in mind, cultivates the question, 'What's best for *them*?' – solid foundations for a highly esteemed church.

Letting go

In a similar vein, releasing the gift calls for non-coercive leadership. If the new community is to be given over to the recipients, the ecclesial hierarchy cannot take the gift back by controlling how it is used.

> "The ecclesial hierarchy cannot take the gift back"

Instead of chaining the new community to others' expectations, leaders must release members to be themselves in Christ.

This does not mean an abdication of leadership. It suggests a particular type of leadership, based on communal discernment with 'small mouths' and 'large ears.'

Recognizing that God's word is too immense to be uttered by one mouth or even one group of mouths, leaders should encourage the community to listen to the Spirit through its relationships with God directly, with the world, with the wider church and within the community itself.

By questioning, correcting and holding one another to account, a chorus of distributed voices can fill every corner of the church, limiting the abuse that may arise from pulpits of power.

Receiving the gift

When the gift is accepted, recipients are drawn into the entire body of Christ. For giving the church to others is more than the offer of one particular Christian community. It is an offer of fuller life within the whole communion of saints.

Failure to offer the complete gift would limit the church's generosity. You'd be holding back part of the gift, which would be at odds with the total self-giving of the church's head.

So God's people must make the fullness of church a practical reality. They must clear paths from the new community to the church at large. They must ask:

- How well does our denomination, diocese, synod or network help new Christians to flourish in their faith?
- Where are the opportunities for new believers to contribute to the wider church?
- How welcoming are the church's structures and processes, especially to people short of confidence?
- Is the greater church being made a pleasing gift to vulnerable people on society's edge?

Giving back

Receivers of the new community will offer the church return gifts that include experience, wisdom, expertise, and knowledge of 'good practice.'

These gifts will not be accepted unthinkingly, aping 'managerialism' outside the church, but in the context of spiritual discernment.

In particular, by challenging harmful habits of thought and behavior, new Christian communities can be prophetic voices to the rest of God's people.

Birthed among people outside the church, these communities can speak on behalf of those the church leaves out. They can help to improve the gift for them.

Transformation

When church and world draw together through their exchange of gifts (but without God's people losing their distinctiveness), the Spirit enables the two to bring out the best in each other.

The church's gifts of solidarity with the weak, care for creation, contributions to the creative arts, and sharing the good news help the world to enjoy a richer life.

Equally, the world's gifts of criticism, advice, and know-how help the church to repair its internal life and become more desirable. Giving the church becomes transformative – to others, yes, but also (just as important) to the church.

What's the bottom line? Each phase of the giving process goes beyond hospitality and contains the seeds of church reform.

As these seeds sprout and blossom, dare we pray that they will display – against all the odds – a people who are an authentic foretaste of God's coming reign?

3. PRACTICING GENEROSITY

What does full-throated generosity look like when you offer community with Christ to others? I believe that the Spirit has bequeathed the church a gift-based methodology to match our gift-based theology.

The missional journey

It is captured in the diagram below, which we call the missional journey. This journey has become influential over the past 15 years among founders of new Christian communities because it describes what frequently happens on the ground.

LISTEN — LOVE — COMMUNITY — SHARE JESUS — CHURCH — REPEAT

Underpinned by prayer and connection to the wider church

> For example, in Bradford, England, *Sorted* is a Christian community among teenagers who are now young adults. It emerged in a series of overlapping stages.[25]
>
> - **Listening.** First Andy Milne and the team got to know young people in the local school.

---

[25] Andy Milne, *The DNA of Pioneer Ministry,* London: SCM, 2016.

- **Love.** Then they introduced fun activities on Friday evenings, with a short Christian input in the middle.
- **Community.** 35-40 young people came regularly.
- **Share Jesus.** Young people interested in God met on another evening. The teenagers decided what would happen in the 'chilled time' (eg computer games), while Andy would bring a discussion topic for 'chat time' (eg God, life issues, a Bible story).
- **Church.** The team began a worship service for those who were becoming Christians.
- **Repeat.** Andy started *Sorted 2* in a different area and then *Sorted 3* in the same area (with the help of some from *Sorted 1*).

Of course, real life is more messy than a diagram, and so the circles often overlap or pile on top of each other. Sometimes they are taken in a different order and teams return to an earlier stage.

Even so, time and again founders of new Christian communities travel this journey. Often they are not aware of it; they act intuitively. Only later do they realize that the path they travelled has been generalized into a journey others are on too.

Propelled by generosity

What is striking is the gift-and-response dynamic that underpins the journey. Each circle is a gift, which elicits further generosity in reply. And that response then becomes the basis of the next gift.

So, for example, 'listening' is a gift that may call forth a generous response of information, ideas, and a willingness to help. These form the basis of 'love.'

Generous 'love' elicits the gifts of engagement, relationship, and trust that form the basis of 'community.'

The generous offer of 'community' elicits the gifts of enjoyment, gratitude, increased trust, and deepening relationships. These create a spiritual openness that paves the way for 'sharing Jesus.'

The latter, we pray, leads to gifts of joy and fresh insights into the gospel from the kingdom's recipients. These return gifts become building blocks for 'church' – a new Christian community connected to the wider body.

This in turn elicits a response of enthusiasm and gratitude that encourage the journey to be repeated, but in a different way for the new context.

Generosity begets further generosity as the church is passed on from one stage of the journey to another, from one corner of society to the next, from God's heart to human hearts.

This is light years beyond hospitality!

4. KEEP GIVING

Remember: a gift only remains a gift if it is passed on. Otherwise it becomes a possession. And the church is never to be a human possession.

We received the church as a gift.

    We are called to make it a gift.

        Let us keep giving the gift away.

DISCUSSION

1. What in the book has most warmed your heart?
2. What has most challenged you?
3. How might your thinking have changed through the book?
4. Is there something you feel called to do next?

Printed in Dunstable, United Kingdom